The World of the Etruscans

The World of the Etruscans

Text by
Aldo Massa
Translated by Anthony Werner

Tudor Publishing Co
New York

Table of Contents

Frontispiece: *Sculptures on an Etruscan burial stele (Bologna Museum).*

© *Editions Minerva, S.A., Genève, 1973.* — *ISBN 0-8148-0579-5*

1. At the Dawn of Civilization

A great variety of peoples, most of which have left only a vague imprint on history, has passed in succession over the territory of Italy. We are told of Aborigines, Ligures, Ausonians, Japygians, Siculi, Oenotrians, Umbrians, Italiots, Pelasgi, Etruscans, etc. But to which peoples did these names refer? How were these peoples different from one another? To which races did they belong? Where did they come from? In what order did they follow one another? How far did they intermix? There are a great many questions which science has not yet answered.

Yet there has been no lack of theories, each more ingenious than the last. But all this wisdom and imagination has produced only improbable, and often fantastic, solutions.

Thus, the Etruscans, whose origin is still unknown, have been successively assigned to all races and countries. They have been described as indigenous Italians, Slavs, Basques, Celts, Canaanites, Armenians, Egyptians, Tatars, etc. Some have agreed with Herodotus that they were Pelasgo-Tyrrhenians who had left the coasts of Lydia and arrived in Italy by sea. Others, like Dionysius of Halicarnassus, have claimed that they were a tribe which originated in the Rhaetian Alps. But no-one has succeeded in penetrating the mists surrounding the past of this enigmatic people. Scarcely any more is known about the other peoples who shared the territory of Italy with them.

One can only indicate the major routes which they took to arrive there. These routes were not chosen arbitrarily: they are governed by the geographical conditions of the Peninsula.

One of them opens out to the North. The valleys which lead down from the Alps to the plains of Lombardy have always carried hordes of invaders into Italy, and history—the history of modern times, the Middle Ages and Antiquity—tells us what must have happened in the prehistoric era. When the great migrations of the Aryan races through Europe took place, this human tidal wave, spreading from the Caucasus to the Atlantic, reached Italy at the same time as Greece: the affinity between Italiots and Hellenes is known. As soon as they had come down from the mountains, the immigrants proliferated in the region of the Po ; then, in a slow and continuous push, they advanced step by step to the Apennines, crossed them, and subsequently progressed as far as the Tyrrhenian

Sea. In outline, this route was the one taken by all the invasions from the North.

Another route was open to the migrations—that of the sea. Italy protrudes so far into the Mediterranean that the first vessels to lose their way in the Ionian Sea were bound to come across it. The sailors of Phoenicia and the Archipelago soon came to know their way around these coasts, upon which they had first been cast by the wind and to which the lure of gain subsequently drew them. They went to the bottom of the Adriatic, to the mouth of the Po, seeking amber from the Baltic and tin from the British Isles, brought there by trade caravans. They went from bay to bay, peddling the wares of their country and engaging in all kinds of barter. They must be imagined like the Phoenicians described by Herodotus at the beginning of his History: they arrived, unloaded their cargo and spread it out on the sand, as in a bazaar, before the covetous eyes of the natives. Then, business completed, they got back into their boats. But, since it was rare in those times not to be a bit of a buccaneer, our good merchants often loaded together with the rest of their baggage a laggard woman or two, who then became merchandise and were sold further on as slaves.

Many of these sailors were merely itinerant. But some stayed on and founded trading-posts of a sort which, by attracting newcomers, ended up by becoming small colonies. The old legend of Aeneas landing at the mouth of the Tiber, the fabulous stories by Herodotus of the Lydians' crossing into Italy, the myth of Circe holding the Greeks spellbound by her charms and making them forget their homeland, the traditional account of the founding of Cumae in the 11th century, the founding of Carthage in the 12th century and later the prodigious development of the Greek colonies in Sicily and what was known as Greater Greece—all these are sufficient evidence of the continuation over centuries of a wave of seaborne migrations to the West and the Italian coasts.

Thus, over many centuries whose history has not been written, Italy was continuously enriched by people who came from all parts, by land and by sea. What became of the meeting of so many different elements, both foreign and indigenous? Sometimes, the original occupants made way for the immigrants; sometimes favorable cir-

A Phoenician merchant vessel (sculpture from Sidon).

cumstances enabled the two races to merge, and the contact of customs, habits and industries gave birth to a new people.

Although only distant and confused reminders of all these populations remain, the soil of Italy still bears traces of their passage or their sojourn. The cities in which they lived have not always disappeared without trace. In many places, their dead are still there, at the site where they were buried, together with some of the objects which pious custom enclosed in the tomb. All this has been sought with care, gathered up and preserved. The number of finds has increased.

The word *terramare* (kitchen midden) is a popular term in Italy to describe certain mounds of rich earth containing bones, shards, coal, organic wastes often found in the Po valley. These were long used by the peasants as marl-pits from which they obtained excellent fertilizer, until the time when they were found to contain remains of human dwellings and the sites of prehistoric settlements. Since then, excavations have made it possible partially to reconstruct how these primitive villages must have looked.

Most of them were situated near watercourses, on earth which if not swampy was at least subject to frequent flooding. They were therefore constructed on piles. They were surrounded on all sides by a fenced embankment which served both as a dike and a rampart. Within these surrounds, vertical stakes—the remains of which can still be seen—were driven in, in parallel lines. They were connected by horizontal crosspieces which supported a plank covered with mud flooring. On this scaffolding rose the huts, which were conical in shape and were made of clay and small matted branches. Thus, the inhabitants lived on terraces, with an open trench always below their feet, into which they threw a jumble of broken instruments, left-over food and all the household garbage. When the trench was filled with refuse, the embankment was raised and new stakes driven in to raise the level of the terraces: in some places, this operation seems to have been carried out at least three times.

The bones of domestic and wild animals, tool fragments, weapons, pottery and scrap of all kinds collected in the terramares gives us a glimpse of the kind of people that inhabited these villages. Despite their apparently lake-

A bust of Apollo was found during the early digging at Veii.

side habits, they did not fish, for what fish could have survived in their muddy trenches? They were hunters and shepherds. They found plenty of game, especially deer and wild boar, in the forests which at that time covered Italy and from which they obtained the wood for their piles. The fields bordering rivers offered pasturelands for livestock husbandry. They had cattle, sheep, goats and many pigs; the pig was already what it is in Italian farms today—the domestic animal *par excellence*. In addition, they farmed some fields of corn, barley and flax.

Their industrial capital was poor. At first, it comprised stone weapons and instruments, but these were vestiges of an earlier civilization which was beginning to disappear as metalworking became more advanced. It later comprised bronze weapons and instruments: these were the most numerous. Bronze was the only metal then known to the people of the terramares and they worked it very badly. All they were able to do was to pour it into stone molds, several of which have been found and all of which are fairly crude. In this way, they made scythes, daggers, hammers, spearheads, awls and hatchets.

9

10

The pottery of the terramares is still rather crude. Most of the vases are of brownish clay, poorly molded by hand, which was never kiln-fired, the outside surface alone having been exposed to a hearth fire: as a result, it is very unevenly baked and has very low resistance. Some vases have a finer grain but are still of elementary manufacture. Many have no handles and were carried by a rope wound round the vase and prevented from slipping by a few small button-shaped projections. Sometimes, the "handle" is merely a hole through which the rope could be passed. The most curious kind, of which most examples remain, is that of the half-moon handle: it is found wherever the men of the terramares lived. The decoration of all these pots is confined to a few geometrical designs drawn on the still wet clay with a pointed instrument: these are mainly crosses formed by a series of lines and points.

Settlements on piles are found only in a specific area of the Po region. But the civilization which their refuse reveals to us was much more widespread. Traces of it have been found in other parts of Italy, quite far from the Po, notably in Latium. Some miles from Rome, in the territories of Albano, Marino and Grotto Ferrata, in the mountainous region which once constituted the volcano of Latium, the necropolis of Alba the Long has been discovered and excavated; its oldest tombs contained pots similar in all respects to those of the terramares and especially remarkable by their crescent-shaped handles. They include several cinerary urns shaped like conical huts and imitating the wickerwork of the huts which served at the time as dwellings: this is the first and the most naïve expression of a very old belief which was to persist throughout the ancient world—the belief that death is not the end of everything for man, that the body, even reduced to ashes, continues a shadowy existence below ground, that the tomb is a dwelling-place and that it must be made to look like a house.

The second group of prehistoric finds which we have to consider after the terramares is the so-called Villanova group. The name comes from a place a few miles from Bologna, where its major characteristics were first determined following the discovery of a cemetery containing about 200 intact tombs.

The Villanovan civilization flourished mainly in the Po valley. There, it occupied an area bounded in the West by the Panaro, a tributary of the Po, and in the East by the Adriatic; this area extended over part of Venetia. It was here that the largest and richest cemeteries, those of Este and Bologna, were found. But the same civilization existed beyond the Apennines: in central Etruria, at Poggio Renzo near Chiusi (Clusium); in coastal Etruria, at Cerveteri (Caere) and especially at Corneto (Tarquinii); in Latium, on the territory of Alba, and in Rome on the Esquiline Hill.

The most characteristic object of the Villanova age is the cinerary urn. Its shape can best be compared to that of a deep bowl on which an upturned pail has been placed. There is usually a single handle at the point where the urn's belly is broadest. The neck is closed by a cover which is itself nothing else but a cup, or rather a small inverted bowl. The clay from which these pots are made differs little from that of the fragments found in the terramares. However, its grain is more

compact and it has been molded with greater care. The surface is not varnished but polished and glazed. The ornamentation is always geometric. It consists of horizontal bands each made up of 2 or 3 parallel strips, between which there is a row of dots, stars or crosses, or a succession of triangles, or else a winding design of varying complexity. All this is hollowed out with an awl. These ornaments never cover an entire vase; they are divided into two separate areas, one at the top near the neck, the other in the middle of the belly. This is no doubt a figured reminder of the many-colored pieces of cloth, lengths of string or strands of wool which were originally used to hang the vases or merely to decorate them.

This urn, thus decorated and topped by its cover, served as a container for the dead person's ashes. It was placed in a square or hexagonal trough, the bottom and sides of which were covered by stones or large pebbles placed flat and forming a drystone wall. Other smaller vases and some of the dead person's belongings were placed all around.

These objects were very varied. Firstly, they included a great many

Motif from a very old Etruscan stele.

Below: fragment of the pediment of a temple.

small clay cylinders, rather like our spools and doubtless intended for the same purpose: a tomb like this would contain up to thirty of them. Small clay cones, which are believed to have served as weights to stretch the thread during weaving, are sometimes found together with these spools. The peoples of Villanova were therefore engaged in growing and working with flax and hemp. It should be noted that the Bologna region, which is where these peoples mainly developed, is still renowned today for its hemp and its rope manufacture.

Weapons are rare: the custom was not to bury them with the dead person, perhaps because the small size of the tomb was unsuitable for this purpose. The arms found in these tombs are miniature weapons, small axes for example, doubtless manufactured with funereal purposes in mind. In the same way, in Greece, light, flimsy jewelry was made for tombs, with only the appearance of real jewels.

The peoples of Villanova loved horses. Hardly any of the richer cemeteries does not contain at least one bit, and often two, as well as buckles, hanging spheres, sometimes small bells and various metal pieces formerly fixed to the harness leather, and the goad with which the team of horses was pricked: this was a pointed sleeve which was fitted over the end of a stick.

The Villanovan burial-places are dominated by objects related to the costume and toilet of men and women —bracelets, necklaces, small chains, pins, blades and fibulae. The blades and fibulae deserve special attention. The blades are thin crescent-shaped strips decorated with ornamental geometric lines; the handle is very short and can only be held with two fingers. The fibulae are pins whose point is protected with a hook, rather like a safety-pin. There are countless numbers of these: as many as thirty are sometimes found in a single tomb, suggesting that the normal attire comprised several. There are various kinds:

Etruscan cinerary urn (Berlin Museum).

14

the curved part is sometimes a simple piece of bronze wire, sometimes a twisted one, sometimes an extruded sheet of metal shaped like a gondola and with ornamental geometric lines. When it was a simple piece of bronze wire, it often had threaded on it colored beads of glass, bone discs, beaver-tooth or amber, or even a piece of amber as large as a pigeon's egg.

The metalware of Villanova represents a considerable advance on that of the terramares. Iron was already known, though little was available and it was still too rare for making bracelets. The bronze industry was very advanced. The metal was no longer cast in crude steel moulds; men knew how to hammer it, flatten it into thin sheets, cut it into discs or strips, chase it with ornaments, bend it, twist it, stretch it and make it into flexible wire. The objects mentioned above give some idea of the skill with which it was worked. Many others could be mentioned, too —knives, awls, handsaws, spearheads, arrowheads, belt-buckles, and in particular buckets made from bronze sheets joined and riveted together, with a lined bottom for better resistance to the weight of the water, and two mobile handles attached to different points so

Statuette of a woman, from Orvieto.

that when the bucket was carried its movements were always counterbalanced. This metalworking is well known in detail today through the discovery in 1877 at Bologna of a large earthenware jar full of broken bronze pieces, unfinished or imperfect utensils, workshop waste and cakes of metal from the hearth. This was clearly a foundryman's store. It weighed almost 3,300 lbs. and contained about 14,000 pieces, including all the kinds already yielded by the Villanova burial-grounds. The total number of fibulae was 2,397.

The Villanova civilization—which it is impossible to date—flourished in Italy over a long period. Obviously, it did not remain stationary. The burial-grounds found at the gates of Bologna were situated in such a way, and the objects shown in museums are classified in such a way, that it was possible on the spot and is possible today before the display-cases to trace the route which it took.

Left: Statuettes of a woman and a warrior, dating from the 6th century BC (Florence Museum). Below: Bas-relief of a burial urn (Volterra Museum).

2. The Etruscan people and its mystery

The civilization which has been called Etruscan was born between the Tiber and the Arno. It was in this uneven region, criss-crossed by the foothills of the Apennines, on ground rich in metals, among numerous fertile valleys sloping gently down to the Plains of Maremma, which at that time were cultivated, flourishing and open to maritime trade, that the industrious Tyrrhenian or Etruscan people lived. This people, which had its own traditions and annals, used to recount how it had settled in Italy several centuries before the founding of Rome, about the 11th century BC. This is not the place to discuss its claims nor seek to discover how it took possession of the Tuscan countryside. Probably, through circumstances we do not know about, a mixture of races, similar to that from which all great peoples in history have emerged, took place. Whatever happened, it is an established fact that a very long time ago, perhaps as far back as the 10th century, the Etruscans formed the basis of a nation, organized as a kind of confederation of twelve cities. This confederation had a political life of about seven centuries. All-powerful in the heart of the Peninsula, it gradually extended its domi-

nation: to the north, where it pushed its conquests beyond the Po ; to the south, where it crossed the Tiber and occupied Campania; and to the west, where its fleet conquered Corsica. It reigned over the new city of Rome. Then came the day when its fortunes declined. The rich cities of northern Etruria — Tarquinii, Caere, Veii — gradually lost their importance to Rome, which, through its geographical situation and also its policies, had become the real trade center, the capital of the region. Soon the confederation had to fall back on all its frontiers. The Greeks drove it from Campania, and the Gauls from the Po basin. Thrown back into central Italy, it was subjected to attacks by Rome and finally succumbed. Its political role ended in the 3rd century, after the Samnian wars.

It is understandable that the civilization of a people which occupied such a prominent place in Italian history should be of such interest. Yet we can see this civilization around us: it has left a great many objects behind. The valleys in which it once flourished, uninhabited ever since the Pax Romana isolated them, have maintained the traces of the past almost intact.

View of the Tuscan countryside from the Etruscan ramparts at Volterra.

Many discoveries have been made in the cemeteries of Vulci, Chiusi, Corneto and Cerveteri, to mention only the main ones.

What were the characteristics of the Etruscan civilization? What causes and influences helped to shape it? One thing is immediately clear: this civilization has nothing in common with that of Villanova. A comparison reveals different customs, a different industry. The arrangement of the burial-ground, the funereal furniture, the shape of the objects, the decorative motifs—everything is different. Two influences in particular, of which there is no trace in the Villanovan finds, are evident: those of Asia and Greece. Etruscan art is nothing more than a combination, in varying degrees of originality, of elements taken from the East, on the one hand, and from Greece, on the other, until the latter finally prevailed and almost entirely eliminated the former.

It is a fact that has long been recognized and which nobody would any longer dream of contesting that, a very long time ago, the East had a powerful influence on the inhabitants of Tuscany. But how was this influence exerted? Who served as the intermediary between Italy and the East?

If the evidence of antiquity, all of which is consistent except in one case, is to be believed, the intermediary was a small tribe of emigrants who set out from Asia Minor and landed at the mouth of the Tiber. This is the tradition which Vergil used and embellished with public fiction. Herodotus relates how in the reign of Attis, in other words towards the end of the 15th century BC, Lydia, which was then the largest part of Asia Minor, was afflicted by a terrible famine. Rationing had to be introduced. Only enough was left to eat every second day, and the people organized all kinds of amusements and games on the days of fasting in order to forget their hunger. Eighteen years passed in this way until the King concluded that there was no solution and resigned himself to sending half of his subjects abroad in the care of his son Tyrrhenos. They embarked and, after long wanderings, finally arrived in Italy.

This tale is full of legendary details, but not all of it is fable. If we subtract whatever may have been added by the popular tradition of the Lydians, gathered and amplified by Herodotus' fertile imagination, the fact remains

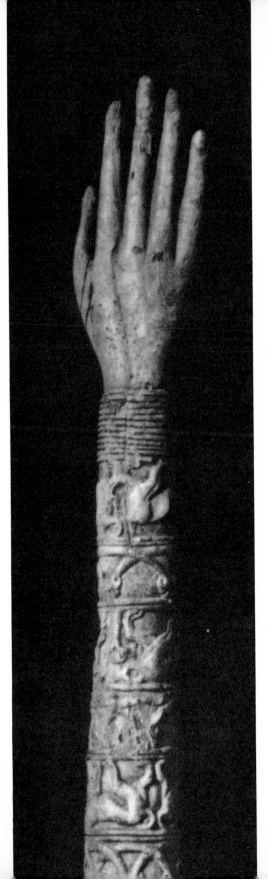

*Sculptured   arm
(6th century BC).*

that there was an emigration which for many years drew off the surplus Lydian population far from Asia Minor. In addition, it is certain that towards the 14th century there was an extraordinary movement of peoples in southeast Europe and south-west Asia. Numerous tribes, driven from their countries by the same human pressure which thrust the Dorians into Greece, wandered over the Mediterranean world looking for a new homeland. Egyptian hieroglyphs describe invaders who landed at the mouth of the Nile with women and children, occupied the entire Delta, settled there and could only be driven from Egypt by strenuous efforts and after terrible battles. It is possible that the vestiges of one of these migrations, after landing on many different shores in this way, may have ended up by being cast upon the coasts of Italy.

Until new and decisive scientific proof is available, the journey of an eastern tribe to Tuscany will remain a hypothesis. But it must be admitted that this hypothesis explains a great deal. For example, it helps us to understand why the same kind of burial-grounds can be found in Etruria as in Asia Minor, mounds resting on enormous tower-shaped substructures and tomb exteriors hewn into the living rock of the mountainside; why the system of vaults, which is oriental, is found in Mediterranean countries only among the Etruscans and the Romans, who got it from the Etruscans; why the Etruscans, alone of all Mediterranean peoples, cultivated the oriental art of soothsaying; why they wore oriental clothes, long flowered robes with glittering edging, Lydian sandals and hoods which recall the Phrygian bonnet; why the royal insignia which the Etruscan family of the Tarquins borrowed from Etruria were the insignia of the kings of Lydia; and why the games and shows of Etruria were of Lydian origin. All these constitute a set of Asiatic customs which appear to relate to the most intimate and earliest traditions of the Etruscan nation.

Perhaps we will never know what to believe. Two scholars — one an Italian, Pallettino, the other a German, Altheim — in fact advanced the argument, some twenty years ago, that there was much too much concern with the origins of the Etruscans and that it would be wiser to consider the data relating to their formation, as is commonly done for the great modern peoples.

In any event, it is beyond doubt that central Italy imported goods from the East through its Mediterranean trade. A tomb at Vulci, known as the Grotto of Isis, contained objects clearly brought from Egypt, such as decorated ostrich-egg shells and flasks of blue glazed earthenware similar in every respect to those found by the thousand on the banks of the Nile. Elsewhere, besides these small flasks, some of the statuettes which the Egyptians placed in tombs in accordance with the funeral ritual have been found; the hieroglyphs which they bear attest to their origin. These are only small objects. But there is an example of an import that is remarkable in quite a different way: a treasure-store of Phoenician objects discovered in 1876 at Palestrina (Praeneste). Among the precious vases which constitute the bulk of this treasure are cups of carved and gilded silver, similar to the decorated cups which have been found in Cyprus, Citium, Larnaca and Amathonte, made in the same way and, like them, of the mixed type, half Assyrian, half Egyptian, which characterizes the products of Phoenician industry.

These facts and many other similar

ones establish the existence of trade relations between the East and Italy. These relations began in a far-off era, when the sailors of Tyre and Sidon, driven out of the archipelago by the growing expansion of the Greco-Pelasgic race, moved to the West, about the 11th and 10th centuries BC. But they developed mainly after the founding of Carthage (middle of the 9th century). From this time onwards, the Tyrrhenian Sea—generally speaking the part of the Mediterranean between Sicily and Spain—may be said to have become a Phoenician lake. The crossings were so well guarded and the Phoenicians so jealous of their possessions in north-west Africa that it could only be entered by surprise. At the end of the 7th century, when Neko II, the King of Egypt, wanted to reach those coveted areas, he had to seek a different path to the normal route and send an expedition from the Persian Gulf, which sailed round Africa and, after a three-year voyage related by Herodotus, returned to Egypt through the Straits of Gibraltar.

Italy was thus surrounded by Phoenician settlements. Its markets were then flooded with the products of the East —gold, silver, ivory, precious stones,

26

dyestuffs, jewels, caskets carved in relief, decorated plates and all the goods of Asia and Africa, not to mention the countless forgeries produced in Assyria and Egypt which Phoenician ships peddled across the Mediterranean. The best stocked markets were of course those of Etruria. Apart from the fact that the Tiber and its tributaries provided ready-made channels for trade to the very heart of the Etruscan country, the Phoenicians in Carthage, guided by their commercial instinct, preferred to deal with the powerful and rich peoples living in central Italy. The trade relations between the Carthaginians and the Etruscans in time became close enough to lead to treaties. We know from Aristotle that they concluded agreements "on alliances and reciprocal rights". Being equally threatened by the advance of Greeks into Southern Italy—one group in their trade, the other in their domination—they united against the common enemy and drove them back from Lilybaeum and Corsica. In the 5th century, Hieron of Syracuse still faced their combined squadrons before Cumae.

The period of Phoenician-Carthaginian imports to Etruria lasted almost three centuries, and the Etruscans' development did not remain unaffected by this contact with the oriental world. Asiatic-style objects widely scattered throughout the country served as models for native workers in the manufacture of bronze tools, jewelry and rings. Above all, they provided decorative motifs. The oldest works of Etruscan industry are little more than designs taken from the flora and fauna of the East; rosettes, palm-leaves, closed or flowering lotuses; wild animals: lions, tigers or panthers, sometimes walking in line, sometimes fighting, sometimes devouring their prey; and fantastic animals or monsters: sphinxes, griffins and winged bulls.

The oriental style lasted for different periods in different areas. In the Plains of Maremma and at Tarquinii and Caere it soon disappeared in the wake of the all-powerful influence of Hellenism. At Vulci and Clusium, on the other hand, it continued for a long time. But it left its mark everywhere in the Plains of Maremma and in Upper Etruria. In the Roman era, Tuscan art still used decorative motifs derived from the East. Palm-leaves, rosettes and lotus flowers can still be found on mirrors and cinerary urns of the 3rd century BC. Sphinxes, griffins and lions guard the peace of the grave in accordance with oriental custom.

But strong as the effect of the East on the civilization of Tuscany was, the decisive influence was that of Greece.

The relations beween Italy and Greece go back to remote antiquity. The two countries are so close that it is hard to believe that sailors from the Ionian Islands and the Gulf of Corinth did not land on the Italian coast early on. The well-known myths of Circe, the Sirens and Scylla and Charybdis, which belong to the most ancient traditions of Greece, are evidence of adventurous expeditions thrusting deep into regions of the West as yet unexplored. The number of these expeditions certainly increased at the time when the Greco-Pelasgians of the archipelago began to challenge the Phoenicians for possession of the Mediterranean, i.e. towards the end of the 13th century BC, when that great empire was established in the Cyclades, an empire which is preserved in men's minds in the legend of Minos, which was mentioned by Thucydides in his history and which had an expansive force to which Egyptian hieroglyphs bear witness. In times of old the Greco-Pelasgians were credited with founding several cities in Italy: Adria, Spina and Ravenna on the Adriatic, Agylla and Caere on the Tyrrhenian Sea, not far from the mouth of the Tiber. Cumae was also regarded as having been founded in the 11th century by sailors from Euboea.

Although all of these tales can be disputed, it is nevertheless certain that the Hellenic emigration to Italy began well before the historic era. But this movement really gained strength only from the 8th century onwards. Rhegium, Sybaris, Croton and Tarentum, and in Sicily Naxos, Syracuse, Leontium and Hybra were founded; later, in the 7th and 6th centuries, Gela, Himera, Selinus, Agrigentum, Paestum, Locris and Metapontum were established. The whole of northern Italy was surrounded by an almost continuous line of Greek cities. The way was now open for Hellenism, which gradually—without invasion or upheavals, by slow infiltration and the all-powerful attraction of its genius—won over the Italic peoples who had so far been exposed only to Phoenician influence. The transition was to be particularly smooth because at that time Greek civilization was itself completely permeated by the East.

With regard to Etruria itself, we

Typical Etrurian hills.

known that it was in direct contact with Greece from the 7th century onwards. The story is told of Demaratus, a royal member of the Bacchiad dynasty who was driven out of Corinth by the usurping family of the Cypselides and fled to Tarquinii, a city in northern Etruria, where he married, became an important official and founded a family whose descendants ruled Rome as the Tarquins. It is likely that a royal exile like Demaratus did not arrive in Etruria by chance, like a poor emigrant who leaves without knowing his destination and lands where he may. He went to settle where other Corinthians had gone before. Etruria, at that time Phoenician, must have been known to the Corinthians, who more than any other Greeks maintained relations with the Phoenicians: their city had long been a Phoenician station in Greek waters, and at the time we are considering they still traded extensively with Phoenicia. Tarquinii was probably inhabited at the time largely by Corinthian settlers and, like its neighbor Caere, which had a treasury at Delphi, was regarded as a Greek city. In any event, these two cities and the surrounding region were won over to Hellenism in the 6th century.

Greek civilization was thus brought to Etruria early on by settlers. But it was primarily trade imports that spread it and caused it finally to predominate. The Greek colonies in Italy, linked by continuous trade to their metropolis, were storehouses from which the products of Hellenic industry were spread by active coastal traffic all along the Tuscan shore.

The most important of these imports were painted vases, commonly called Etruscan, but not so in reality. Some were made in Etruria, but these were either carefully wrought works made by Greek artists living in the country and thus to be regarded as purely Greek, or else clumsy imitations, worthless forgeries. It may be said that most painted vases found in Etruria came from Greece. It was there that the main workshops were situated, and it was there that all this beautiful pottery, sometimes signed by the same artist, which has been found at the two ends of the Mediterranean—in Crimea and in Tuscany—originated.

Imports of pottery to Etruria lasted for a long time. All styles are represented in Etruscan cemeteries: the Corinthian or Asiatic style which flourished in Greece in the 7th and 5th centuries; pots with a red background and black figures (end of the 6th and beginning of the 5th century); pots with a black background and red figures (5th and 4th centuries). The Etruscans seem to have had a special preference for these objects. The burial-ground of Vulci, discovered in 1828, contained about twenty thousand pots.

Like the Phoenicians, the Greeks were untiring merchants, and the reason why they marketed so many and such beautiful painted pottery in Etruria is that they found a rich and guaranteed clientele there. Thus, it can be said with certainty that they did not confine themselves to that class of objects, but brought many other products of their industry, which was already flourishing in the 6th century.

Greece flooded Etruria with its works. It gave it not only its industrial output, but also its alphabet, its mythological figures, its legends, currencies and artists. By the 7th century it was already tradition that among Demaratus' companions were two artists, doubtless two potters: Eucheir (= he who has a fine hand) and Eugrammos (= he who draws well).

Later, in the 5th century, we shall encounter the names of two more Greeks, Gorgasos and Damophilos, who worked in Rome and were probably summoned, there from Etruria.

Decorations on an Etruscan tomb. Right: Achilles, on an Etruscan terracotta sarcophagus.

Etruscan bronze helmet, dedicated to Olympia by Hieron of Syracuse after a battle against the Etruscans (6th century BC).

3. History of the Etruscans

Very little is known about the history of the Etruscans. Since the works written on the basis of their annals have disappeared, and those annals themselves left little mark on the memory of antiquity, we have very few texts, which only refer to Etruscans in passing and which, apart from being very few in number, are mostly not sufficiently explicit to give an overall historical picture. We must confine ourselves to a few facts and a few dates marking the major periods of the political grandeur and decadence of Etruria.

The Etruria of old, the Tuscany of modern times, constitutes only part of the territory once occupied by the Etruscans. It is there that they mainly developed, that their political activities were centered and that their most important cities were established. But it was not their sole domain.

Traces of their stay in northern Italy can be found. Livy, who came from Padua and whose testimony deserves special attention here, writes that the area between the Alps and the Apennines had belonged to the Etruscans. He also states that there were Etruscan tribes in Rhaetia.

The Etruscans are found again along the shores of the Picenum, in the territory of the Praetutii and the Palmenses. Atria Picentina recalls the name of the Etruscan city of Atria and the town of Cupra is named after an Etruscan deity.

There were also Etruscans beyond the Tiber, in the country of the Volscians and in Latium. Fidenae and Crustumina are referred to as Etruscan cities. The name Tusculum is a diminuitive of Tuscum. The name Velitrae (Velletri) is reminiscent of Velathri (Volaterrae). Tarracina seems to be another form of Tarchna or Tarkina (Tarquinii). Although the Roman legends about the time of the last kings are not at all precise, it seems that from the time of Tarquinius Superbus to the overthrow of the monarchy Rome was more or less an Etruscan protectorate. It had taken in, probably about this time, a number of Etruscan settlers and still maintained an Etruscan Quarter *(Tuscus vicus)*.

The territory of Campania was also occupied by Etruscan tribes. According to Polybus, at the time when the Etruscans were masters in the Po basin, they also held the territory known as the Phlegrean Fields, where the towns of Nola and Capua, which were said to have been founded by them towards the end of the 9th century, sprang up. Sophocles refers to Lake Aornos, near Cumae, as being in Etruscan country. According to Pliny, Dicaearchia, Puteoli, Herculanum, Pompeii, Surrentum, Marcina and the entire *Ager Picentinus* up to the river Silarus were in the hands of the Etruscans.

The Etruscans were therefore spread out over most of Italy. They even advanced as far as Corsica and perhaps Sardinia.

The Etruscans early on had a political organization, which also explains the development of their power in Italy. According to the little that remains of their national legends, this organization was born in Tuscany, in that part of Tuscany closest to the sea and the Tiber, in the territory of the Tarquinii, which seems to have been a kind of metropolis. It was said to have been fathered by the hero after whom the city is named—Tarchon, son or brother of Tyrrhenos. One day when he was working, a spirit, the spirit of Tages, had appeared to him in the shape of a child and had revealed to him the principles of the sacred discipline and the science of divination. Inspired by this supernatural wisdom, he gave

Hunting scene (Volterra Museum).

Etruria its religious constitution and thereby its political constitution, since politics and religion formed a single entity for the ancients.

To become well acquainted with this political constitution we should have the *rituales libri* of the Etruscans, which contained, *inter alia,* all the provisions relating to the distribution of inhabitants by tribe, curia and century, the organization of the army and all things connected with war and peace. Unfortunately, these books left only confused and scrappy traces in the minds of ancient peoples. But, by gathering a few sparse details from the authors, we can glimpse the principles on which Etruscan society was based and how it was governed.

This society was essentially aristocratic. The term *principes* recurs constantly in the texts when Etruria is mentioned: it is the equivalent of an Etruscan word transcribed by the Latins as *lucumo* or *lucmo.* These lucumos had a dual function which was both political and religious: they were priests and leaders at the same time, as can be clearly seen from a text of Censorinus which states that Tages' sacred discipline was gathered and written down by lucumos. They thus consti-

Bronze vase-stand (6th century BC).

37

tuted a privileged order which, because it possessed the hereditary right of knowing and interpreting the priestly code, was the only one qualified to manage public affairs. The lucumo families in Etruria were no doubt akin to the Roman *gentes,* but with the difference that in the Roman aristocracy women did not count, so to speak, whereas in the Etruscan aristocracy they had equal status with men. Nobility was not transmitted only from male to male; there was also a nobility for women. Unlike the custom in Rome, in a great many Etruscan epitaphs the mother's name is a title of honor added to the patronymic. The legend of Demaratus is very significant in this respect. He was a foreigner, an exile from Corinth: but his marriage to a woman belonging to the Etruscan aristocracy was enough to insure that his children were noble and belonged to the family of the Tarchnas.

Just as the Roman city was a federation of *gentes,* so the Etruscan city seems to have been a federation of lucumo families. These families, together with their clients, formed a number of religious groups corresponding to what was known in Rome as a curia. Festus mentions Etruscan curiae and

Etruscan warrior attacking a fortress (burial-urn decoration, Chiusi Museum). Below: Etruscan warrior (terra-cotta, 5th century BC, Metropolitan Museum, New York).

Servius tells us that the Etruscans of Mantua were divided into twelve curiae. Several curiae together formed a broader group, corresponding to a tribe: at least, this can be inferred from a text by Varonius which states, quoting an Etruscan writer Volnius, that the names of the three tribes of primitive Rome—Ramnes, Luceres and Tilies—were of Etruscan origin; Festus also mentions tribes in Etruria. There were certainly three such tribes, as in Rome, and this number corresponds to the tripartite division governing the founding of any Etruscan city, which could not be correctly established unless it had at least three sanctuaries and three gates. According to Servius, there were three tribes in the Etruscan town of Mantua. It is difficult to say exactly what the *centuriae* mentioned by Festus as existing in Etruria were—military and political or territorial divisions.

Nothing suggests that the structure

of Etruscan society remained the same down the ages. Like all other peoples, the Etruscans must have had their revolutions. However strong an aristocracy may be, there comes a time when it is forced to reckon with the demands of the people which it has been accustomed to dominating and which has been increasing in numbers while the aristocracy itself has been declining and wearing itself out. That is a human law with which the Etruscans complied even more because of the fact that their country early on became a center of trade and industry; it is impossible that greater wealth should not, in the longer term, have changed social conditions, not to mention the fact that the democratic spirit of Greece must have spread quite easily among peoples who were daily brought closer to Hellenism by constant contact with Greeks in Campania and Tuscany.

The migration of the Tarquins to Rome, the adventures of Mastarna and Celes Vibenna, which are mentioned by the Emperor Claudius in his speech to the people of Lyons and some episodes of which are depicted on a fresco at Vulci, show that in the 7th century BC, just at the time when central Italy was beginning to throw itself wide open to Greek goods and ideas, Etruria was going through a period of domestic upheavals and discord. The reforms of Mastarna, who had become king in Rome under the name of Servius Tullius, seemed to indicate by their democratic leanings that a new spirit had permeated Etruria and that the old aristocracy of the lucumos had been, if not overthrown, at least breached. This led to the troubles in Veii at the beginning of the 5th century BC, which are mentioned several times by Livy and which brought about changes in the form of government through the replacement of an elected royalty by magistrates holding office for one year, and the subsequent return to royalty. One may even wonder whether the political decadence of Etruria should not be attributed in large measure to the revolutions which divided it at this time.

We do not know the exact form of government in each Etruscan city. A good many texts mention the existence of kings in Etruria, including Arimnestos who erected an ex-voto to Olympus, Porsenna, the famous king of Clusium, Tolumnius, Propertius, Morrius and Thebris, king of Veii. But were they really kings in the full meaning of the word? May not the title of king, in the

41

mouths of the Latin and Greek authors using it, have been a fairly accurate equivalent to denote the supreme magistrate of a city? One thing appears certain: there was no hereditary royalty in Etruria. The kings of Veii were elected. As far as can be conjectured, the head of an Etruscan city had to be a kind of elected prince, appointed for life by the members of the lucumo families and doubtless from among the lucumos, rather like the first kings of Rome, who were elected by the patrician Senate and governed together with it. Like them, the Etruscan king was assisted by a council of lucumos, whom authors liken to the Roman Senate. And as in royal Rome, it seems that there were popular assemblies.

Just as the Etruscan city was a fede-ration of curiae, so the Etruscan empire was a confederation of cities. They were twelve in number, a figure doubtless sanctioned by certain religious theories, since there were also twelve curiae in Mantua. Everywhere that the Etruscans organized themselves into a political body there can be found a dodecapolis—in Tuscany, north of the Appenines, in Campania.

At the time of the Empire, when Etruria was no longer independent and formed part of the Roman domain, the symbol of the province was still the dodecapolis, which was represented on the quadrangular plinth of the monument to Claudius, one of the faces of which was found at Cerveteri. The confederation of twelve Tuscan cities, of which Tarquinii seems to have been

42

the capital, is the only one on which we have some information, and even this is not very clear. We do not know for sure either the names of the member cities or the extent of the territory of which these cities were the capitals. If we take all the texts together, we arrive at a total of not just twelve but seventeen cities in Tuscany, all having a about the same qualifications for being included as federal cities. Probably, over the years, as some towns declined while others prospered, the capitals of the twelve regions did not always remain the same.

As a guide, we shall list the names of the twelve cities which are regarded today as most probably having made up

the confederations. They are Tarquinii, Veii, Cerveteri, Volterra, Cortone, Perugia, Arezzo, Voisinii, Clusium, Vulci, Vetulonia and Rusellae.

Joint affairs were managed by a council similar to the Greek amphyctiony. This council's meetings, like those of the amphyctiony, where held in a sanctuary, the temple of Voltumna, the location of which cannot be determined with certainty but which seems to have been in northern Tuscany. Regular meetings were held annually, in the spring, but extraordinary meetings could also be convened at the request of one or more cities, which sent deputies to the other cities for this purpose.

Left: Etruscan gate at Perugia. Opposite: Duel between leading Etruscans (Archaeological Museum, Florence). Below right: Countryside around Volterra.

Not much remains of Etruscan cities. They were covered, and often damaged, by Roman and then medieval buildings, and the modern era itself has not always respected them. Where the cities have been left alone, the erosion of centuries has done its work. These cities were almost always built near a river and on top of a hill. The main ones were not far from the sea: Vulci, Tarquinii (the oldest city of Etruria) and Caere (today Cerveteri). Veii was

once famous for its waters and Volterra was certainly an important city, too, because its ramparts, which have fortunately been preserved, were almost six miles long.

The most spectacular development of the Etruscans occurred between 700 and 600 BC. At that time they followed immediately after the Greeks as far as civilization was concerned. Towards the end of this period, the Tarquins (of Caere) annexed and controlled the Roman areas. They were to lose them in 509, but at the same time the Etruscans advanced in the northern regions of the peninsular: after Bologna, the cities of Parma, Modena and Mantua were founded, as well as Spina, on the Adriatic, and Melpo, not far from the site of the present city of Milan.

In 474, the defeat of the maritime expedition at Cumae, which was regarded as an akward rival, marked a turning-point in Etruscan history. About seventy years later, war broke out between Rome and Veii; Livy devoted the major part of two books of his History to this conflict, which lasted eight years and ended in a Roman victory. Veii's prosperity at the time was the envy of the Romans, Livy reports, and their booty exceeded

their wildest Bologne, dreams.

The confederation made itself felt again in 307 by a small expedition against Carthage, but two cities soon went over to the powerful Romans and an irreversible—at least politically irreversible—decline set in, for the Etruscans, like the Greeks, who were themselves conquered by Rome, were to understand the way in which their "wild conqueror" could be conquered.

Defensive wall built by the Etruscans at Rome (called the Servian Wall after Servius Tullus). — Two Etruscan warriors.

48

4. The land and the towns

Having occupied part of Italy, the Etruscans found themselves spread out in various kinds of country, some of which, like the "Maremman Plains" of Tuscany, were unhealthy areas. We know about some of their sanitary engineering work.

For example, they had tried to use diversions, dikes and canals to regulate the Po estuary and the mouth of the Arno. They had made outlets for the dormant underground watercourses of ponds and lakes by digging drainage channels; everywhere, in the towns and in the countryside, they had built artistic drains and sewers. A curious example of these is the Graviscae drain.

As a result of this hydraulic work, the country began to flourish. Population centers were numerous and prosperous. Around the towns, each of which was built on healthy heights and was defended by solid ramparts, lived a whole world of industrious artisans, each with a plot of ground. Agriculture was highly esteemed. The earth, rich and well drained, bore fine cereals, and the fertility of Etruria was proverbial. The Maremman Plains, in particular, sent part of its corn to Rome. Cereals were also abundant in the Chiana and

Po valleys, around Perugia, Clusium, Arretium and Pisa: the *far* of Clusium and the *siligo* of Pisa had a good reputation. According to Virgil, agriculture was Etruria's strength. The oldest legend of Etruria, that of Tages, which is intimately linked with the political and religious civilization of Etruria, derives from agricultural life; in addition, the ceremonies which—following a very old tradition—were held when a town was founded include the tracing of a sacred furrow by a plough in accordance with a certain ritual at the place where the walls of the new city were to be erected.

Cereals were not the only produce of Etruria. There was a lot of flax and hemp around Tarquinii, because at the time of Scipio's expedition against Carthage, that town alone supplied all the sails needed by the Roman fleet. Not far away, near the Tiber, excellent fishing-nets were made; Falerii, too, was renowned for its linen cloth.

The olive-tree and the vine flourished. An inscription at Vulsinii refers to the olive-trees bordering the fields around. Vines grew strongly enough for a statue of Jupiter to have been made of a vinestock at Populonia. Columella notes that up to two thou-

Vergil among his muses. Below: Etruscan bronze (6th century BC).

49

sand grapes were gathered from a single vine-stem at Caere. The wines of Tuscany, while inferior to Campanian wines, had some worth, especially those of Luna and Graviscae.

The Apennine heights, at that time less bare than they are today, were covered by forests which provided an abundant supply of materials for maritime and civil engineering. These were also available in certain parts of northern Tuscany. Etruscan pine was famous. Scipio's fleet was built of wood from Perugia, Clusium and Rusellae. The best roofing used in Rome came from Etruria.

Etruria does not seem to have been a country particularly well endowed with pasturelands. But it did have some, because livestock was bred in parts. It is certain that there were plenty of horses. Tombs often contained bridle-bits and various harness and saddlery pieces. Phaleran horses were used in Etruria before they came to Rome. The Etruscans' public games almost always included harness or mounted horse-races, as a great many funeral paintings show. The Etruscan cavalry seems to have been quite well-organized at an early stage.

As well as horses, oxen—needed for work in the fields—were raised in Etruria. The hardiest were those in the Apennines. Falerii produced a fine species of white bulls, which were much sought after in Rome for sacrifices.

We also know that the Etruscan peasants had sheep. References were made to Tyrrhenian wool and ewe's

The famous fresco on the "del Barone" tomb at Tarquinia (6th century BC).

cheese from the Apennines and especially from Luna, which was sold with a stamp of origin. Lastly, it must have been rare for an Etruscan farm—like Italian farms today—not to have had pigs and bees. The pigs wandered in herds, guided by the sound of a trumpet. Beehives were found in plenty in the Volterra area.

In addition to all this livestock, the Etruscans also hunted and fished. The authors mention Tuscan boar, and hunting scenes were often depicted on monuments. Several paintings also show fishermen at work. Pyrgos is referred to as a fishing center; Populonia and Cosa had observation posts to mark the passage of tuna fish.

Judging by what remains of Marzabotto, near Bologna, the streets of Etruscan towns were arranged crosswise around two main avenues, one running north-south and the other east-west: these avenues were about 45 feet wide, and the streets were about 15 feet across.

Houses were generally built in the same way: in the center was the *atrium,* a kind of small courtyard off which all the rooms opened. It was always open in the middle: rain was channeled into a small tank along four weather-boards sloping towards the interior, which also protected the rooms against heat. These weather-boards could be adjusted in various ways, as was to be the case later during the Roman era. In Etruria, the rafters of which they were made were usually supported by two main beams running

51

parallel and forming a kind of horizontal bridge from one wall to the other. This is what the Ancients called the *cavoedium tuscanicum.*

It is difficult to imagine the exterior of an Etruscan house. Several burial urns depicting houses suggest that there were few openings to the outside, and that a covered balcony, similar to the *loggia* which many Italian houses still have today, was sometimes built under the roof.

Around the atrium, which was a meeting-place for the family and clients, were grouped several rooms, each no doubt with its own special purpose, as they later had in Rome. The walls were perhaps sometimes decorated, as were the burial-chambers, either with embossed-metal ornaments or with painted ceramic plaques. Furniture was plentiful and sometimes luxurious: there were fine sculpted beds, covered with soft cushions and glowing with color, as can be seen from the sarcophagi and paintings; trunks decorated with metal ornaments; armchairs, tables, three-legged stools, candelabras of embellished bronze, dressers on which stood beautiful Greek vases or gleaming bronze, gold or silver plates. There was no lack of carpets and rich

Interior of a tomb at Cerveteri.

Fishing scene: decoration on a tomb at Tarquinia (6th century BC). Below: Urn from Vulci depicting a house (7th century BC).

wall-coverings, to judge by the many-colored fabrics depicted in the paintings and on the sarcophagi. In addition to all this, there was an abundance of equipment and accoutrements familiar to any warlike aristocracy, all of which can be seen on the reliefs of the *dei Rilievi* tomb at Cerveteri. All the household objects of a rich Etruscan are depicted in their natural state, as if really hung along the walls, in this tomb: casseroles, jars of all shapes and sizes, bags, wallets, boxes, pliers and other tools, straps and harnesses.

Etruscan candelabra (Archaeological Museum, Munich).

Caponic jar (Florence) and recep-
tacle dating from the 8th century
BC (Vatican).

57

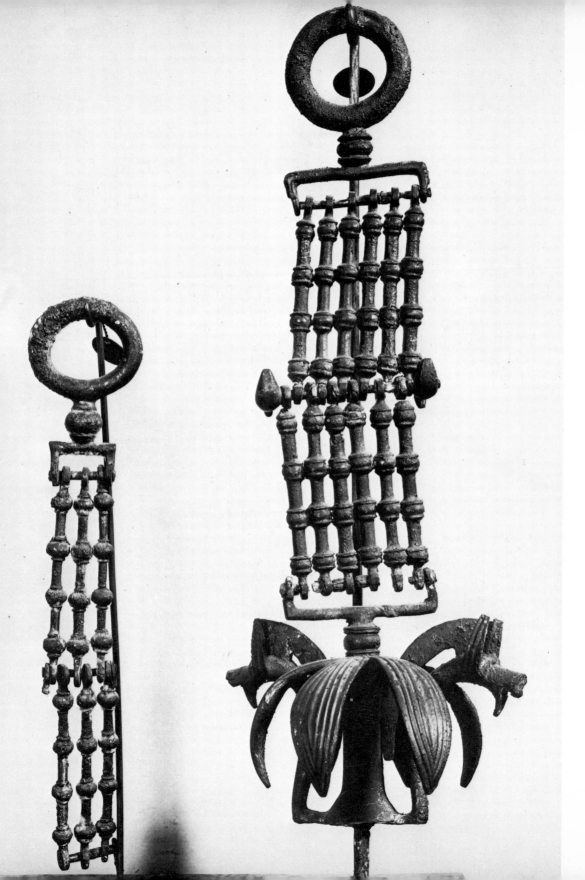

5. Trade

Although the part of Italy over which the Etruscan tribes were spread was destined to become, and did indeed become, an agricultural region, it was also, by virtue of its geographical situation between two seas, in the Mediterranean world and in continental Europe, to become a commercial meeting-point. Greek and Phoenician sailors, plying the coasts in search of adventure and profits, were bound one day to have arrived on Adriatic shores and at the Tyrrhenian coast.

The first Etruscan foreign transactions were localized at the mouth of the Po valley. This area was referred to at a very early period as one of the major markets for amber. It was the terminus of one of the caravan routes along which amber was brought from Germany through Central Europe; it was here that merchants from Phoenicia and Greece came to buy it. We shall not describe or discuss the traditions regarding the origins of and trade in this amber. Suffice it to say that several of them cite the northern Adriatic as the region of origin of the precious substance, indicating that there was a sort of depot there, as in indeed confirmed by archaeological discoveries: it is rare in the very old tombs of the Po valley area not to find some fragments of uncut or worked amber.

We do not know how long this amber trade at the mouth of the Po lasted, or whether it was always active and vigorous. What is certain is that towards the 9th century BC trading in the Mediterranean tended to move gradually away from the Adriatic and to veer towards western regions. The founding of Carthage marked a new era in this respect. The seaborne activities of the Phoenicians were now increasingly concentrated in the Tyrrhenian Sea and spread to the coasts of Western Italy, Gaul and Spain. The movement started by the Phoenicians was soon followed by the Greeks, who were motivated to follow in their footsteps by constant rivalry, and a wave of maritime migrations now began, bringing all the adventurers of Greece, the Archipelago and Asia Minor to Italy over a period of several centuries. The extraordinary spread of Greek colonies in the West is well known.

It was inevitable that one day or another the Etruscans of Tuscany would have to enter into close relations with this world of foreigners. Although

Lampstands of the 8th century BC (Vatican).

access to the shallow waters of their coasts was usually difficult, the merchants of Carthage and Greater Greece gradually became accustomed to stopping there and trading. Trading-posts were set up, even settlements, which spread their goods further and further into the heart of the country by river or by means of the great religious festivals.

The existence of trade with Carthage is beyond dispute. There were treaties between the Carthaginians and the Tuscans. Since, for a trading people, political alliances always lead in the end to commercial alliances, we can be sure that these treaties were drawn up so as to serve the interests of the Tyrian merchants and that they enabled them to market their goods in Etruria. There is also plenty of archaeological proof to support this theory. Up to the 7th century, tombs often contained objects from the East, and some tombs dating from about the 7th century—for example, the so-called Grotto of Isis at Vulci, the Regulini-Galassi tomb at Cerveteri, several tombs at Palestrina, the *Del Duce* tomb at Vetulonia—show that at a certain point, as a result of circumstances which are difficult to explain, Phoenician-Carthaginian trade

predominated in Tuscany.

At this time, imports consisted of gold and silver jewelry, silver or ivory plated boxes, bronze cauldrons with griffins' heads, gilt-silver goblets with Asiatic-style carvings similar to those found in Cyprus, ostrich eggs decorated with wild fantastic animals—in brief, a rich variety of precious objects whose origin is incontestably clear from their entirely Eastern decoration.

But however much Phoenician-Carthaginian trade in Tuscany may have flourished at a particular time, it was only of passing importance. The Etruscans depended above all on Greek trade. From the time when the Chalcidians, apparently the first Greeks to have organized emigration to the West, settled in the territory of Cumae in the 8th century, up to the final conquest of the Mediterranean world by the Romans, it may be said that the Greeks did not stop doing business with Tuscany for a single moment. The details of this business are not known: we shall confine ourselves to noting the Greek peoples who played the greatest part in it.

Firstly, there were the Chalcidians and their settlements at Cumae, Rhegium and Naxos, which in turn dotted

the coasts of Campania with settlements. In all probability, it was they who brought the art of writing to the Etruscans. There is every reason to believe that some of the bronze objects found in the oldest Tuscan tombs are of Chalcidian origin.

About the same time, the Phocaeans were spreading out across the Tyrrhenian Sea. The founding of Marseilles at the end of the 7th century must have made a special contribution to the development of their trade with Tuscany, and it may perhaps have been in order better to protect these trading interests that they settled in Corsica, from which the Carthaginians, helped by the Etruscans, later forced them to withdraw. Phocaean money pre-dating the second half of the 6th century has been found in some parts of Tuscany.

Then came the Corinthians, whose expeditions to the West closely followed those of the Chalcidians and whose relations with Etruria are shown in the

Left: Iron firedog. Above: Ornaments on a vase. Below: Receptacles (7th and 6th centuries BC).

legend of Demaratus coming to settle in Tarquinii, after the usurpation of Cypselos, with a party of the Corinthian aristocracy.

At the beginning of the 5th century, the monopoly of Greek trade with Tuscany seems to have been held by the Corinthian settlement in Syracuse. Until the last century, the prevailing view was that this monopoly belonged to Athenian merchants, and the vast amount of Attic vases found in Etruscan burial-grounds do in fact seem to bear out this contention. But the scholar Helbig has shown that there were no real direct relations between Athens and Tuscany, and the reason why Etruria was full of Attic products is that they were brought there by merchants from Syracuse.

About the 3rd century, after the decline of Syracuse's power and the final collapse of Athenian trade, Etruscan markets fell into the hands of the towns of southern Italy, especially those of Campania. From this time onwards, almost nothing else is found in Tuscany but objects of Campanian origin or style, and a large amount of coins from Campania. There was, then, a double trade flow between Tuscany and Greater Greece—partly by sea along the shores of the Tyrrhenian Sea, partly inland, along the roads built across Italy by Roman engineers, the Appian Way and the Latin Way. The existence of this inland transport is evidenced by the commercial and industrial importance which was now assumed by the city of Praeneste, near the Latin Way, in the valleys leading, on one side, to the Tiber and Tuscany, and, on the other, to Campania.

Were the Etruscans content to accept the goods brought to their shores by foreign ships, or did they, too, have a merchant fleet to fetch the products of Carthaginian or Greek industry from afar?

The question is difficult to answer. If ancient traditions are to be believed, the Etruscans were enterprising and formidable sailors. The bad reputation of Tyrrhenian pirates is well known. But it is not certain that these famous pirates were Etruscans from the Tuscan coast. There were Tyrrhenians in Thrace, Asia Minor and the Archipelago, and there is nothing to suggest that the generic term "Tyrrhenian pirates" was not used to denote the whole group of adventurers who sailed the seas of the West, engaging in trade

and piracy at the same time—Phoenicians, Carthaginians, Phocaeans, Chalcidians and others, rivals but bent on avoiding any appearance of competition and concerned to make themselves feared in order to insure that they had a monopoly over their operations. However that may be, it is beyond question that at one time the Etruscans had a fleet. But it is probable that the commercial role of this fleet was confined to plying along the Tuscan coast and that it hardly operated in Greek waters, where the jealous Greek merchants would not have gladly put up with competition.

Chariot and figures on a burial urn.

64   *Ornamentation on the "Scudi" tomb at Tarquinia.*

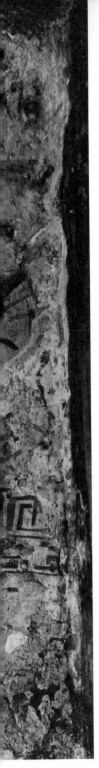

6. An art of living

Gabriele d'Annunzio made the Etruscans fashionable at the beginning of the sixth century by his drama *Forse Che Si, Forse Che No,* the action of which takes place in Volterra. His characters believe that they understand the message of the first Etruscan inhabitants of the city: everything in life boils down to Anxiety, Sadness and Fatality. In 1932, the famous English novelist D. H. Lawrence in turn drew the attention of the public, in his *Etruscan Places,* to the ancient civilization with which we are concerned, but in a completely different way to that of the Italian poet.

The author of *Lady Chatterley's Lover* saw the Etruscans as epicures, even sybarites, unaware of it but clearly so. They left phallic symbols everywhere, which Lawrence seems to have regarded as an intentional plan. The Etruscans had found faith in life, they accepted it joyfully, they overflowed with vitality, while at the same time being "delicately sensual": in their paintings, when a man caresses a woman, his caress is beautiful because he *knows* how to touch. There is an entire poetry of contact between human beings in the Etruscans. They also lyrically describe the "natural flowering

of life", which is not as simple as it seems: "At the heart of its ardor lay a religion of life... behind all these dances was a vision and even a science of living, a concept of the universe and man's place in it, which made them live to the very fullest. To the Etruscans, everything was alive and it was man's duty to live too. He had to absorb in himself all the life of the world." Lawrence contrasted this art, this science of living with the principles of the Romans, who hated the phallus because they wanted domination and wealth: "One cannot both dance gaily to the sound of the double flute and conquer the world".

In the 4th century BC, the Greek historian Theopompus had a similar idea of the Etruscans, but an infinitely less delicate and profound one. He described Etruscan women as "common to all men"! This absolute calumny (although he would not perhaps have regarded it as such) was decked out with various details: Etruscan women took great care of their bodies, played at gymnastics, either with men or by themselves, in the most simple clothing. They reveled and caroused with anyone. They did not know who had fathered their children. Making love in

public did not brother them at all. Prostitutes and young men procured for homosexuality were legion. After banquets, the Etruscans all made love "watching each other" (unless they had reed screens put up—as they sometimes did—around their festive beds).

It must be said that such stories were widespread at the time: authors as different as Plautus and Horace and the great Aristotle himself took them as gospel truth. They were certainly exaggerated, but they show that the Etruscans, at least, knew the art of living well and loved "the good life". They had no literature, no maxim to shed light on the question, but we have their numerous works of art, which speak volumes: Lawrence seems to have understood and assessed them correctly, without in the end denying the sense of the innate tragedy of life on which D'Annunzio, contemplating the number and importance of Etruscan tombs, may perhaps have dwelt at too great length but which may in the final analysis explain the intensity of the Etruscan "carpe diem".

Etruscans went bareheaded and wore sandals with simple laces. Women, however, sometimes wore curious high-

These burial-urn lids and two busts (terra-cotta), below right, are very evocative.

Right: Fibula (Vatican Museum, Rome). Following pages: Heads of a young man (the same as that shown opposite in profile) and of a mature man (Villa Guilia Museum, Rome).

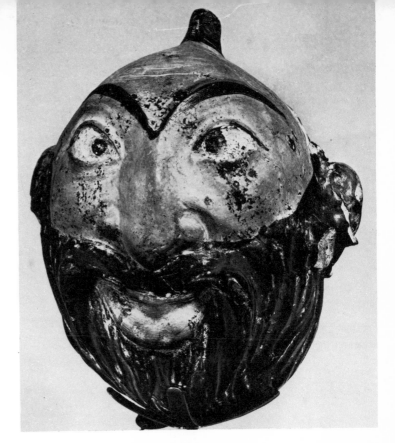

Left: Bust found at Cerveteri, dating from the 4th century BC. Right: Rhytons (drinking horns) with caricatures (4th century BC, Etruscan Museum, Rome).

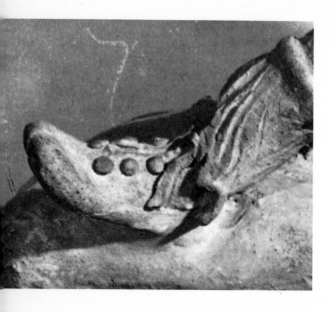

sided, ankle-length Greek-style shoes.

The luxury of toiletry and finery was extreme. Etruscans liked to wear vividly-colored clothes with purple bands, flowered motifs and embroidery. Hairstyles were very elaborate and, like the entire costume, showed the influence of Eastern fashion.

The lid of a ceramic sarcophagus shows the care with which the smallest detail of attire, hairstyle and adornment—in brief, what we would call accessories—were depicted. Some folds of fabric are so soft that they give the impression of the fabric itself. The various cloths used in the costume can be distinguished by their thickness. Every hair is perfectly in place. The artist has depicted everything—the decorated hood, the sandals with their

Model of Etruscan sandals, from a figure on an urn (Vatican) and folds of a dress from the same source (Archaeological Museum, Florence).

Above: A man's hairstyle (Flo-rence).

straps, the embroidered belt fastened under the breasts with its ends falling loose, the brooches, the necklace with pendants, the earrings, the floral tiara, the bracelets at the wrist and elbow, the rings weighing down the hands and encumbering every finger-joint, the mirror bordered by a double row of pearls.

The Etruscans liked good food. The ancients described their sumptuous meals, which were served twice a day, and in which the women, "intrepid drinkers", sat next to the men, greatly scandalizing visiting Greeks or Romans, who were used to seeing only courtesans seated in this way at feasts.

Diodorus Siculus says: "They prepared superb meals. They reclined in front of sophisticated dishes served in silver plates on flowered tablecloths".

Numerous frescoes show us the Etruscans at table, surrounded by slaves hurrying to serve them. Everything exudes cheerfulness, and more than one picture suggests by the complete abandon of the poses that the exuberance of the guests was not without a degree of licentiousness. These meals kept a large kitchen staff busy. Paintings on a tomb at Orvieto show us all the preparations and almost enable us to reconstitute the different parts of the menu.

The frescoes often depict a man and woman reclining on a bed, heaped with covers and cushions. They are both clothed in brilliantly-colored fabrics embellished with various designs and embroidery, which add further glitter. Sometimes there are three beds instead of one, each with a couple—this is a *triclinium*.

A group of musicians and dancers was an essential accessory. Men, naked or wearing a short coat, played the lyre and danced at the same time. Women played the castenets. Sometimes together with men and sometimes standing apart in a straight line, they wheeled, jumped, turned and curtsied like ballerinas. They wore a dazzling costume, a long gown of light transparent cloth, covered with small designs, and over it a kind of shawl of thicker and darker material. Their hair, neck and arms were laden with jewelry.

Etruscan dances could be religious in nature. Livy relates that they were introduced to Rome as such during, of all things, a plague: "To appease the gods, the idea of staged games was conceived, something quite new for a

race of warriors accustomed only to amphitheater games. Artistes from Etruria danced as they do in their country, accompanying themselves on flutes. This kind of spectacle spread and the actors were called *histriones* after the Etruscan term *hister*."

Festivals were held often, and games and hunts even more frequently. The walls of burial chambers show wrestlers, discus-throwers, gladiators armed to the teeth, horse races, chariots ready to sart in the arena or already racing. In one place, a group of horsemen and hunters pursue a wild boar; in another, the boar is brought to bay by the hounds. Further on, two horsemen return from the hunt, preceded by a guide directing them through the woods and followed by a slave carrying the game caught on the end of a pole.

The Etruscans caught stags and boars by heading them off with dogs and then trapping them in nets. According to Elienus, a remarkable feature was that flute-players helped the operation: "The sound of flutes", he writes, "is first heard in silence over the hills and in the woods—when they hear it, the animals are dazed and anxious. Then they are overcome by genuine pleasure and they leave their lairs."

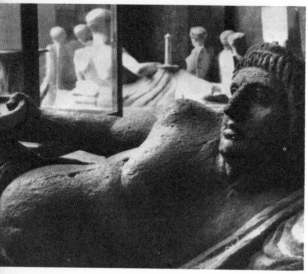

Music accompanied not only the hunt and meals but also many other activities. The instrument in most widespread use was the double flute, but lyres and trumpets can also frequently be seen on tomb paintings.

We have seen that the Etruscan woman was the equal of the Etruscan man, a very rare phenomenon in the ancient world. This is confirmed by the evidence of art: burial inscriptions which mention the name of the dead person's mother as well as the father and frescoes depicting women participating in scenes of public life. Women had similar status only in Lydia.

Although the tales of the Greek Theopompus about generalized prostitution in Etruria are a tissue of calumny, it must be said that cases in which young girls offered themselves for this purpose were perhaps not very rare. But the aim was actually to build up a dowry in order later to marry and thereby to "settle down". For marriage was a respected and much sought-after institution. It was solemnized by an obviously symbolic ceremony: the bride and bridegroom placed their heads together, which were then covered by a veil. From that moment, they were one and the

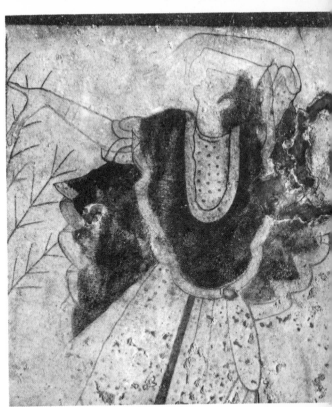

Sporting scenes: bas-relief on a cinerary urn and bronze statuettes. Riding (Tarquinia). The dance (idem).

81

union was indissoluble.

A sarcophagus at Vulci depicts the story of a happy couple. One of the bas-reliefs shows the husband and wife hand-in-hand, each accompanied by slaves bearing the casket, the parasol, the wife's fan, the augural staff, the ceremonial chairs and the husband's trumpet—this is a marriage ceremony. In a second bas-relief, the husband is preparing to enter the triumphal chariot. The last one shows the husband and wife, shaded by a parasol, seated in a chariot drawn by two mules, and the presence of a Fury indicates that the road they are taking is that of the other world: death has not separated them. They have made the final voyage together and rest in the same tomb.

The wife, of course, had to bring up the children and manage the household. But she often took part in business, like Tanaquil, wife of Tarquin the elder, whose ambition and skill, according to Livy, enabled him to come to the throne. After Tarquin's death, she persuaded the people to accept his protégé, Servius Tullius.

All the evidence proves that the Etruscan couple (who are depicted on a variety of occasions arm-in-arm or

holding out their hands to one another) had an infinitely greater concept and habit of tenderness than the Greeks, for example, and many others throughout history. Their children are always shown with them, and it is clear that the family was the basic element of Etruscan society.

Above: a young woman being seized by a satyr.

Faces of women... Bust of a woman... It is curious that, as in the case of the faces of men shown earlier, all these figures on burial urns seem to be of the same age.

7. Knowledge and the arts

The oldest building works found in Etruria are defensive structures. On the hills on which most towns were built one can today still see in several places the remains of powerful encircling walls which are reminiscent of the high Pelasgian walls of Greece.

This system was followed by another in which the transition to greater regularity is already evident. Let us consider, for example, some parts of the walls of Fiesole or Volterra, which appear to be polygonal. Their parts are of different shapes and sizes and do not form a continuous line. But a closer look reveals that all the stones are four-sided and that they are all laid more or less horizontally. If these stones were all made the same height and cut at right angles, the wall would be perfectly regular.

This regular defense wall, the Roman *opus quadratum,* is found in Southern Etruria, at Suti, Falerii, Ardea and Tarquinii, and in Rome, where the oldest walls of the royal period were built in this way. It is the wall of the great times of Greece, but less carefully constructed.

The Etruscans had neither Egypt's granite nor Greece's marble, nor any of the compact rocks which were used to make 18-foot and even 24-foot lintels such as those at Karnak and Mycenae. Since they could not make the ceilings of their vaults from a single block, they used several stones cut in such a way that, when placed side by side, they held each other up and remained suspended in a semi-circle, supported solely by their weight. In other words, they built what we call barrel arches, using, for the first time in Europe, a technique which has since become part of current architectural practice, but one which they did not invent and which was first used in the East: it has been shown that Egyptian and Chaldean architects know of its use a very long time ago.

The Etruscans were not only builders of walls. They also knew how to carry out engineering work. The region in which they lived is only habitable if it is constantly provided with adequate sanitation. There are insufficient slopes in the plains for watercourses, which are plentiful and often large in so mountainous an area, so that as a result they are spread out, lost and end up by becoming plague-ridden marshes. It was therefore essential, above all, to regulate the water system. The Etruscans understood this

Vestiges of Etruscan ramparts at Volterra.

and soon became masters in the art of damming rivers and streams, digging diversion canals, ditches and, as we have already seen, drainage channels, if necessary digging through mountains to provide the necessary outlet for the water. Under the ruins of their towns a complete network of sewers can still by seen, demonstrating the seriousness with which they took public health. These works were extensive, and they can be judged by the work which had to be done to make and keep fertile one of Etruria's most flourishing regions—the Chiana valley, between Chiusi and Arezzo.

The nature of the soil was usually conducive to such work, especially underground work. The bedrock almost everywhere in Etruria is a very soft chalky subsoil easily ploughed up and yet solid enough not to crumble into dust. It was easy to drive underground passages in it. But when the bedrock was uneven, insubstantial and liable to cave in, the passages had to be prevented from collapsing as soon as they were built: this was done by supporting them by means of an artificial wall to counteract the weight of the earth. The simplest method would have been to mount a large

stone beam, such as the Egyptians and Greeks used, on two vertical props.

The most interesting of the vaulted passages which we owe to the skill of Etruscan engineers is the great sewer of Rome *(cloaca maxima),* a magnificent structure built by the Tarquins which was admired by the Romans themselves and which, though repaired several times in days of old, still looks today as it did then. The stones of its archway are dry-joined, as are the elements of all Etruscan walls, without the use of any cement. The arch is made up of three rows of stones, placed one on top of another to strengthen each other, and the opening is so big that, according to Pliny, a chariot loaded with hay could be driven under it.

Etruscan engineers did not use arches only to bridge the walls of their underground passages. They were also used to throw bridges over rivers and especially to let monumental gates into the sides of walls. Several of these gates still exist today, notably in Volterra, Falerii, Sutri, and Tarquinii. The archway above them is built out in relief from the wall front and is usually decorated with curious human heads or Gorgon masks. Whenever a fortified city gate is depicted on burial bas-reliefs it always conforms to this pattern.

The dome-shaped coverings which can be seen at Cerveteri, Orvieto, Cortone and Frascati must not be confused with the barrel arches which have just been described. They are merely false arches. All the stones of which they are built are laid flat, but in such a way that the various rows project successively above each other and the walls therefore come closer and closer and almost touch. The dome is then almost complete and all that is needed to finish it is to round off the protruding corners in a circular or conical curve. A typical pseudo-arch of this kind, called a corbeled arch, is that of the Greco-Pelasgian treasures at Mycenae.

The best-known Etruscan architecture is their burial architecture. Tomb exteriors differed. In the plains we find mounds *(tumuli)* of varying height such as were built in Greece and especially Asia Minor, most of which rested on an enormous cylindrical stone base. Some of these tumuli—the tomb of Cucumella, for example, at Vulci—resemble veritable fortresses. In the hills, instead of making tumuli, the Etruscans followed a custom found in

This famous fresco is at Tarquinia.

More views of the Etruscan ramparts at Volterra.

Egypt and Asia Minor: taking advantage of the terrain, they worked the rocks which lay along the hillsides. In one place, a projecting rock was cut in the shape of a cone or a tower; in another, a sheer cliffside was smoothed out and a series of façades comprising a frame, cornice and door were hewn into it. Elsewhere, the bedrock was cut into one or several archways. When Greek architectural models became popular, the Etruscans even went so far as to cut temple façades out of the rock, complete with pillars, pediments with statuary and all their decorative accessories: the tombs at Norchia were made in this way.

The largest part of an Etruscan tomb was the underground gallery cut into the rock face or made in solid masonry, which was sometimes carefully and artfully concealed at the end of long and deep corridors. Sometimes, this gallery consisted of a single circular or square room of varying size. Sometimes, it comprised several communicating rooms making up a kind of apartment. Some of these rooms were very simple, with only four walls and one or two pillars supporting a ceiling made to look like the beams of a roof, and all around a broad bench on which

to place the bodies. But they were often very ornate. Some were decorated with elegant pilasters, friezes, cornices, panels and alcoves into which the burial beds were cut; others had walls covered with all kinds of joyous or sad paintings; still others depict all the details of domestic furniture in colored bas-reliefs.

No Etruscan temple has been preserved. The few remnants which exist are mostly insignificant. We would have no idea of this religious architecture if Vitruvius, the great Roman architect of Augustus' time, had not described it for us.

Etruscan temples were nothing but Greek temples that had been more or less disfigured. Like them, they had a sacred and private precinct *(cella)*, a colonnaded portico and a façade surmounted by an entablature with statuary, all decorated in various colors. But although the parts were the same, their arrangement was different. The shape of the Greek temple was a more or less elongated rectangle with a naos at the center and one or two rows of pillars either in front of the entrance of surrounding the entire structure. The Etruscan temple, on the other hand, was almost

95

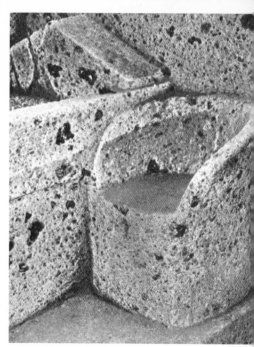

Left: Vestibule of the Etruscan tombs at Volterra whose entrance is shown on the preceding pages. Burial chamber at Tarquinia. Stone chair near the bed on which the body rested. Right: Spirit bearing away the body of a young woman (6th century BC, from Cerveteri. Louvre).
Below: Burial bed found at Cerveteri (Louvre).

square and only had pillars at the front. Its shape and various parts were determined, irrespective of any artistic considerations, by certain rigorous and inflexible religious rules and by astronomical observations. It always had to be made up of two separate halves. One, situated right at the back and forming the rear of the temple *(postica)*, comprised an almost always triple cella enclosed on three sides by a thick wall in which were set statues of deities. The other, situated in the front *(antica)*, was a portico with severals rows of pillars into which the three chambers of the cella opened.

The Greek temple was built from top to bottom in stone. But the Etruscan temple was made almost entirely of wood; only the pillars were sometimes of stone.

These details given by Vitruvius are confirmed by the sculptured rocks at Norchia which depict Greco-Tuscan façades, as well as by several burial urns in the shape of temples.

These same urns show that Etruscan architects modeled their pillars on the Greek Doric, Ionian and Corinthian orders: there are pillars without scrolls, others with scrolls, others with leaf-

decoration which recalls the acanthus. Mention has often been made, and is still sometimes made, of a Tuscan order, separate from the three Greek orders and entirely original, which supposedly arose spontaneously in Italy through the natural development of certain building principles common to the Greek and Italic races. But in fact there is no Tuscan order. The "Tuscan" pillar is nothing but an imitation of the Doric pillar.

Tuscan art started with pottery, and it was here that it was at its most original. The art of molding clay and hardening it by fire goes back to very ancient times in Italy. Pots of various shapes and sizes were made. Improvements were gradually made and new forms emerged, the most remarkable being the *canopes* and the pots known as *buccheros*.

The word canopic derives from Egyptian archaeology, in which it denotes certain burial jars capped by a head. It was carried over into Etruscan archaeology, because the Etruscans often put jars of this kind into their tombs. A canopic jar is a jar for holding the ashes of a dead person. Sometimes—and more usually—the handles had no attachments, ane in this case the arms, shown in rough outline and slight relief, hang at the sides or are crossed over the rounded belly; sometimes they had two arms fitted into the opening and attached by a hook. The fingers are arranged so as to hold an object, for example, a weapon. A curious feature of the heads is the care with which the smallest details of the face, such as the eyelashes, eyebrows and pupils, are shown, and the very oriental evenness of the hairstyle. This

is a primitive concept of the bust, and one is tempted to wonder whether the word *bustum* (something burned) did not originally denote something which was used to preserve both the image of the dead person and the ashes gathered at the pyre.

Canopic jars belong to the first period of Etruscan art (8th-7th century). It was about this time that there emerged the industry of *bucchero nero* jars, so called because they are made of a certain kind of black clay found in Tuscany. A few of them have completely smooth or only slightly fluted handles. All the ornamentation is around the neck, where a single motif is repeated again and again. The themes do not vary much: lines of animals or processions of supplicants walking towards the thrones of the two deities. From the 6th century onwards, the buccheros, which are found in abundance in the Chiusi area, were made in a great many different shapes, often more bizarre than elegant, and with rich relief ornamentation, either molded and hammered on, or embossed: woman's masks, heads of lions or horsemen.

While the potters of Tuscany were thus molding their black clay, Greece

was importing its painted vases. The attraction of this new, light, elegant, multicolored and varied pottery was fatal for the bucchero. In southern Etruria, which was soon Hellenized, the bucchero lasted only for a short time. In northern Etruria, where Greek vases could only be obtained after a costly voyage and long remained luxury items, it lasted longer; but in the 4th century, when even the remotest provinces of Etruria had been flooded with Greek vases and could buy them cheaply, competition became impossible and the bucchero was no longer made.

Now that Greek vases were fashionable in Etruria, as always happens in such cases, attempts were made to forge them. Etruscan potters started to make false Greek vases in order to profit from the popularity enjoyed by the real ones. They made archaic ones—red vases with black figures or black ones with red figures, depending which kind was more sought after.

The Villanovan discoveries have shown how well the oldest inhabitants of Italy were able to use bronze. The tradition continued in subsequent centuries, but changed under the influence first of the Asiatic style, then of the Hellenic. The prosperity of the

Etruscan bronze industry is shown by the fact that its products, mainly lamps and plates, were sought after in Attica at the time of Pericles. In the 3rd century bronze products were exported beyond the Alps, to Gaul and the Danube area. When the Romans took Volsinii in 280, they found and took away 2,000 bronze statues. In 205 BC, when Scipio was preparing his expedition against Carthage, the town of Arretium alone was able to supply him, in a period of fifteen days, with 30,000 shields, 50,000 javelins and all the equipment needed to arm a fleet of 40 ships for war.

A large number of Etruscan bronzes have come down to us. Some are small idols, popular figures of Lares and Penates, and votive statuettes. Some are household utensils: boilers, three-legged stools, ewers, buckets. Others are implements of war: lances, cuirasses, helmets, trumpets, horses' bits, harness and chariot fittings, etc. Still others are luxury domestic items: toilet boxes or cists *(cistes)*, mirrors, fans, lamps, etc.

The cists are cylindrical or oval boxes made of a rolled and soldered bronze sheet. They are often called Praeneste cists because most of them came from that town, but the term is

not quite accurate, because some have
been found at Vulci and in Picenum,
and there is no proof that they were
only made at Praeneste. The name
mystical cists sometimes given to
them is completely unjustified.

Etruscan mirrors are an imitation
of Greek ones. Like them, they are
made of a silvered or gilt bronze disk,
polished on one side so as to reflect
images. Like Greek mirrors, too, they
of two kinds: the double box mirror
with reliefs on the lid, and the simple
disk mirror with handle, decorated
with engravings or *graffiti*. The latter
was the more common type.

These mirrors are interesting because
of the subjects engraved on them.
Some of these subjects are borrowed
from Etruscan life: a mirror in the
Florence Museum, for example, shows
a rustic dance. But usually they
depicted mythological scenes. The
legend of Troy, as told in Homer's
epics, is prominent, the Greek characters sometimes being interspersed with
Etruscan heroes.

The name of the character almost
always appears next to or above it.
We can therefore see how the Etruscans transcribed Greek names: Ulysses
became *Uthuze,* Diomedes *Zimthe,*

104

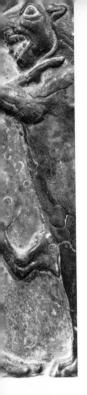

Gorgon, on a chariot fixture (6th century BC, Munich). Cist lid.

Apollo *Apul*, Achilles *Achle*, Castor and Pollux *Castur* and *Pultuce*, Adonis *Atunis*. We can see also which Etruscan deities corresponded to the Greek gods: *Tinia* was Zeus, *Menrva* was Athena, *Touran* was Aphrodite and *Phuphluns* was Bacchus.

Of all the plastic arts, the one which flourished most in Etruria was painting, because of the models offered in their thousands by pottery imported from Greece, and also because of the Greek potters who had settled in Etruria: they brought with them from their workshops in Greece not only the special technique of painting on vases but also the tradition of the great Greek paintings.

All the remaining Etruscan paintings are wall frescoes which decorated burial chambers. Most of them come from Tarquinii. The burial grounds of Cerveteri, Chiusi, Vulci, Orvieto and Veii provide only a few.

The oldest of these works differentiate between men and women by the color of the skin: women are white, men red. All heads are shown in profile, even when the rest of the body is shown from the front and, by a sort of inverse clumsiness, the eyes on all these profiles are shown from the front. But Etruscan art was to improve ra-

pidly: painters would soon be able to render both the forceful contours of a male body and the more delicate shape and slightly hesitant grace of a female body.

A tomb at Corneto depicts a man singing and accompanying himself on the lyre. Instead of one of the immobile and blissfully smiling profiles found in ancient works, we see a lively face: with his half-open mouth and eyes lifted to heaven, the *Cithara Player* really looks like an inspired man giving himself up completely to musical improvisation. The unknown artist who painted this picture must have been influenced by the school of Polygnotus. Polygnotus was the first painter who, the Ancients say, broke with sacred figures and tried to give more life to his subjects' faces by painting their mouths slightly open; he was also the first painter to paint transparent cloth floating round the body.

After imitating the Greeks and their mythological subjects, sometimes adding typically Tuscan details, Etruscan painters were content to depict their contemporaries' games, dances, races and festivals. They discovered perspective, light and shade. They show an urge towards realism, which was often unknown to the Greeks. Sometimes they depicted tragic scenes. There is no need to stress the immense value of their testimony: their frescoes take us into the very civilization of the Etruscan people, into the details of their customs and feelings. We see, as it were, a corner of their lives: we surprise them at table, at the hunt, at the circus, at a funeral, in the midst of their sorrows and their joys. We know all about the luxury of their furniture, their dress, their finery.

Most of the Etruscan sculptures which have been preserved are either in soft stone or terra-cotta. But it is the latter which seems to have been preferred by the Etruscans. This terra-cotta was always painted, for the Etruscans could hardly conceive of sculpture except as multicolored.

In fact, their bronze sculpture was better than their sculpture in stone. The skill of Etruscan artists in manipulating the metal was often praised in ancient times. Today, we have only small bronze items, toilet articles and utensils to judge by. Statues are very few: they include *The She-Wolf* in the Capitol, *The Orator* in the Florence Museum and *The Child with Bird* in the Vatican.

Statue of a king on the ramparts at Volterra.

To appreciate the real value of
Etruscan sculpture we must always
return to works in clay. Clay is found
everywhere in Italy and has been used
for all sorts of work since very early
times. The authors of ancient times
often refer to the terra-cotta statues
made by the Etruscans. The custom
was to use them to decorate the
façades of temples. When the Tarquins
built a sanctuary to Jupiter on the
Capitol, they called in Etruscan artists
who made several terra-cotta statues
and quadrigas for the pediment and an
image of the god for the sanctuary
itself. This monumental work has
disappeared. The wooden temples
have been torn down or burned together with their fragile ornamentation.
The remains of this ornamentation may
one day perhaps be found.

Although Etruscan sculpture has
some merits of accuracy, it is of little
value as art. Its value is above all
archaeological because it brings to life
the customs and beliefs of Etruria.
From this standpoint, the bas-reliefs
on the sides of sacrophagi deserve
close attention. The subjects are often
taken from everyday life.

The industrial arts of Etruria should
be given prominence. We ought also

to deal successively with: *money,* from primitive coins of cast bronze to the coins of beaten gold used in certain towns from the 3rd century onwards, using the Greek coinage system and types; *engraved stones,* especially those in the form of scarabs, the style of which the Etruscans took from Egypt, which they sometimes used as amulets but mostly as seals, and which were partly imported from Phoenicia and Greece, partly made in Italy; and *jewelry.*

Etruscans—both men and women—liked to wear jewelry. This luxury followed them to their tombs. Together with them were buried either the gold and silver ornaments and precious stones which had belonged to them, or flimsy ornaments, simple cut and embossed metal sheets which were mere shadows of jewels. The figures carved on the sarcophagi are always greatly ornamented and depict everything which the dead person owned in the way of jewelry.

The item of jewelry seen most frequently is the bulla-necklace. A bulla is a kind of gold, silver or bronze locket made of two small hemispherical pieces soldered at the edges. It was hung by a ring from the chain of a neck-

Lampstand (Etruscan Academy Museum, Cortone).

lace or from a bracelet. The bulla was one of the objects regarded as warding off evil spirits. It was rare for an Etruscan not to wear at least one bulla. The usual number was three; they were sometimes interspersed with pearls and pendants in the shape of elongated pears. Bullae were still worn by the Romans but only singly, and then only by children who had not yet reached the age of manhood and by conquering heroes.

After the bulla, the jewelry which the Etruscans seem to have favored most was the chain. They had them in all shapes and sizes: double or triple strands; large ribbons comprising four or five rows of parallel strands ending in large rosette-shaped clasps; ring-chains, strings of pearl, stones or pendants.

These chains were endlessly inter-twined, covering the neck, shoulders, breast and hips with metal and giving more the impression of a harness than of an ornament.

The most interesting of all Etruscan jewels from the point of view of their manufacture are those with filigree and grain work, a very delicate process whose secret is still not completely known, and a marvelous example of

Etruscan earrings from Populonia (5th century BC, Archaeological Museum, Florence).

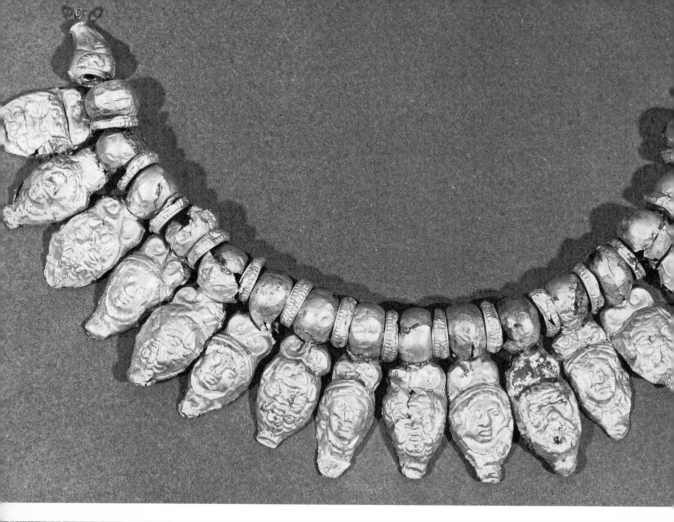

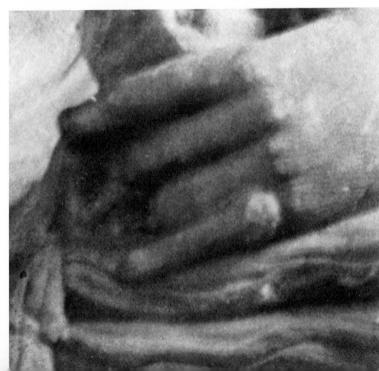

Necklace from the Betollo necropolis (5th century BC, Florence). Pendants (Etruscan Museum, Rome). Opposite: Woman covered in chains and hand with ring (Volterra).

113

which can be seen on a pendant in the Louvre.

The style of Etruscan jewels did not always remain the same. The oldest ones were made according to the principles of oriental ornamentation and reproduce shapes no doubt imported in trading. Examples are the pectoral in the Gregorian Museum and the fibulae with crouching lion or sphinx in the same museum. One of the most widespread models in the 7th and 6th centuries was the "ball" drop earring. Greek tastes predominated from the 6th to the 3rd century, the period to which the finest Etruscan jewels belong. Most of them are wonders of delicacy and elegant fantasy, with a wide variety of motifs taken from animal or plant life and with extremely fine filigree or grain work; some examples are the Bolsena drop earring, a fine fibula disk in the Louvre and another fibula in the same museum.

A great many Etruscan inscriptions have now been found. It is believed that the characters were of Chalcidian origin but included special signs of their own, such as a letter similar to our F which must have come from the Middle East.

All that we know about the grammar is that had declensions. Some Etruscan words have been identified: *leu* for lion, *tin* for day, *lauchume* for noble, *sech* and *clau* for daughter and son and *papa,* not for father but for ancestor.

The modern age, with its strong desire to return to nature, will note with particular interest that Aeschylus called ancient Tuscany "the country of medicines" and that these medicines were plants. The region was rich in herbs and the Etruscans were knowledgeable about their properties. It was also rich in hot springs, the benefits of which had been noted at an early stage.

8. Beliefs

All the peoples of ancient times liked to boast of their piety and each tried to be more religious than the others. But there are none whose claims appear more justified than the Etruscan people. Livy calls them a religious nation *par excellence* and Arnobius says that Etruria is the mother of superstition.

We shall not attempt here to compile a list of gods worshipped by the Etruscans. Firstly, we do not know them all. Secondly, most of the names which have come down to us have been preserved on engraved mirrors dating from the 3rd century BC, a period by which Etruscan mythology had changed radically under the influence of Greek mythology. Lastly, it is almost impossible to distinguish between deities of truly Etruscan origin and Italic gods. What must be determined above all is the nature and spirit of the Etruscans' religion.

The main feature of this religion is that it was based on a kind of divine hierarchy. The supernatural world had several levels.

At the highest level were the mysterious, impersonal and impenetrable deities, whose names, number or appearance nobody could tell, whom none should seek to know, who remained hidden in the depths of the heavens and the undefined nature of whose power made them even more to be feared. They were denoted by vague terms such as "the veiled gods", *dei involuti*, or the "upper gods", *dei superiores*. These abstract and elusive deities were probably identified by the Etruscans with Fate, that anonymous and mysterious demiurge who, according to Suidas (unless that writer added oriental and astrological traditions to Etruscans ones) had created the world for twelve thousand years, each period of one thousand years corresponding to a sign of the Zodiac, and who, it was popularly believed in Tuscany, had assigned ten centuries of existence to the Etruscan nation.

The second rank in the heavenly hierarchy belonged to twelve deities—six gods and six goddesses—who formed a council around Jupiter or *Tinia*. Like the earth, therefore, heaven had its deliberative assembly and a kind of dodecapolis. These twelve gods, whom the Latins called by the generic name of *dei consentes* or *complices*, were identified early on with the twelve gods of the Greek Olympus: in fact, it is very difficult to discover how the Etruscans imagined these deities. Their role was determined by the theory of thunderbolts, a theory about which we know very little and which has certainly come down to us complicated by subsequent astrological theories. Some texts state that only nine of these gods were allowed to hurl thunderbolts, and even then only a certain kind, for the Etruscans distinguished eleven kinds of thunderbolt, of which three belonged to Jupiter.

All this is very complex and obscure. If the texts are accurate, it seems that the *dei consentes* were in fact only minor deities, created and mortal, responsible for maintaining order in the universe but powerless to change anything, armed with thunderbolts not in order to strike men whenever they wished but to announce the supreme decrees of the *dei involuti,* i.e. the decrees of Fate.

The deities of the underworld formed a separate class in the divine hierarchy. They cannot be grouped either with the *dei involuti,* because they have names, or with the *dei consentes,* because they do not reside in heaven and therefore have no relationship with thunder. They were called Mantus or Mania, and are the kings of the underworld. Their role in Etruscan

mythology is similar to that of Pluto and Proserpina, with whom they seem ultimately to have become identified: on a fresco at Orvieto they are depicted with the names Hades (Eita) and Proserpina.

At the very bottom of the divine hierarchy were other supernatural beings, spirits and demons, who lived near men, a sort of mediators between heaven and earth, agents of supreme authority. Their role was to carry out what had been decided. They were of infinite number and were present everywhere. They presided over the birth, life and death of all who were born, lived and died on earth—men, animals, plants. They were called by various names: Penates, Lares, Manes, Genii, but the generic term seems to have been Penates. According to Nigidius as quoted by Arnobius, they were divided into four categories, emanating from Jupiter, from Neptune, from the gods of the underworld and from the human race. As a historian has noted, these categories correspond to four categories of spirits —those of the air, water, the earth and the souls of the dead.

Of these divine ministers, the best known to us through the figured

monuments of Etruria are the demons
of the underworld: the Charons armed
with mallets and torches and the Furies
bristling with serpents which the
Etruscan imagination liked to conjure
up and which are so often found
depicted on Tuscan bas-reliefs and
paintings. Most of them are hideous to
look at and were thought of as male-
volent.

But while this was appropriate for
demons of the underworld, we should
not imagine that all other spirits were
thought of in the same way. Side by
side with these horrible Charons,
whose sole mission was to strike at
mankind, Etruscans believed in the
existence of certain benevolent spirits
which helped and supported them.
There was, for example, the spirit
of Tages who revealed the principles
of religious science to the Etruscans,
thereby giving them civilization and
power; there were the *Lasae* who are
often found on engraved mirrors of the
3rd century, female deities who were
a sort of kindly demons, similar to the
Victories of Greek allegory; and, on
the fresco of the Francis tomb at Vulci,
there is the female spirit standing
behind Achilles and seemingly trying,
by a conciliatory gesture, to restrain

the impatience of Charon like an angel of life protecting from the demon of death, to the very end, the unfortunate Trojan whom Achilles is preparing to kill.

In brief, much remains obscure and unexplained in this mythology whose main features we have tried to describe. At very best, we can only glimpse the general nature of the theological system. This is because the texts are rare, not very explicit and mostly written by late authors who are sometimes mistaken about the meaning of the traditions which they describe, sometimes add rather suspect commentaries and sometimes introduce elements borrowed from oriental philosophy or theology.

While much of the essence of Etruria's religious beliefs escapes us, we scarcely know more about the external forms which these beliefs took. Cults must have been numerous and varied. Only one seems to have been common to all the cities in the confederation, the worship of Voltumna, which was administered by a high priest elected by the federal assembly.

Three basic cults are always found in every Etruscan city, none of which could be properly constituted unless it had three sanctuaries dedicated to *Tinia, Cupra* and *Minerva.* The role of this trinity was similar to that of the Greek polyad divinity, but besides these more or less compulsory cults Etruscan towns usually had one or more cults of their own. At Falerii, for example, there was special worship of *Juno Curitis* or *Quiritis.* Similarly, the main deity of the Etruscan settlers in the *Tuscus vicus* of Rome was Vertumnus; at Vulsinii, the most popular cult was that of the goddess *Nortia,* a kind of Fortuna; at Aurinia, it was the cult of Saturn, whence no doubt the name Saturnia by which the town was later known; at Feasulae and Horta, it was that of *Ancharia*; at Lunus, the cult was of Lunus and Luna, two deities corresponding to Apollo and Artemis; at Capena, it was that of Feronia, during whose festivals, like those of Voltumna, a great fair was held.

The study of these Etruscan cults is greatly complicated by the difficulty of distinguishing what really belonged to Etruria and what was either part of Italic tradition or came from abroad. The worship of Feronia and Juno Quiritis was probably Sabine in origin. The cult of Juno Quiritis also seems to have come under broad Hellenic

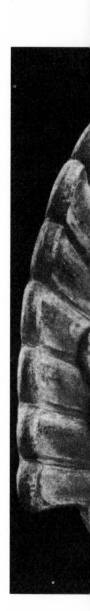

*Figure of an
Etruscan demon.*

influence, for its organization and ceremonies are reminiscent of the Greek celebrations in honor of Hera. Obviously, over the ten centuries or so during which the life of the Etruscan people lasted, its religion changed if not in spirit at least in form.

In view of the relations which had been developed by trade between Etruria and the sailors of Phoenicia and Greece, it was impossible that certain foreign customs should not, in the long run, have been brought to Etruria and been intermingled with the traditions of the local religion. The kind of sacred figures which the people worshipped are of particular significance in this respect. At first, Etruscan idols, like those of primitive Italic peoples, were rather crude symbols, for example, tree-trunks or rough-hewn stones. The Jupiter of Populonia, mentioned by Pliny, was probably nothing more than a vinestock, as were doubtless the ancient images of Vertumnus. Later, about the 8th century, figures from oriental mythology appear in Etruria, Persian Artemis, for example, who was to retain her double pair of wings for a long period, and the Phoenician god Melkarth with a huge head and short legs. Later still, divine

121

figures were almost always modeled on Greek deities, as may be seen from a bronze figure of Apollo, in the Medals Collection in Paris, which is completely Greek in style and attitude and is only Etruscan in its adornment. By the last period of Etruscan civilization, about the 3rd century BC, Greek forms had become so widespread that the originality of Etruscan religion seems to have become lost in a kind of Greco-Italic syncretism. The extraordinary spread of Bacchanalia in Etruria is sufficient proof of the ease with which the Etruscans absorbed and appropriated foreign superstitions. It may therefore be assumed that, on the whole, their sacred ceremonies at the height of their power differed little from those of Greece.

But despite the influence of foreign cults on Etruscan religion, it always retained a characteristic feature: its formalism. No people, not even the Romans, went further than the Etruscans in their concern for, and the art of, sacred ritual. For the Etruscans, everything was related to religion, and they regarded it as a very exact science in which nothing was left to chance or man's free will. The establishment of towns, sanctuaries and altars, the smallest details of political and religious, civil and military life—everything was skilfully controlled with scrupulous care. Every human institution was subject to certain conditions of situation, orientation, form and inauguration which had to be determined through a number of complex operations, based on the theory of the *templum* and observation of certain heavenly signs. Since it was important that the will of the gods should be known as exactly as possible under all circumstances, rules were drawn up to govern the art of ascertaining, grasping and interpreting that will. The reputation of Etruscan divination is well-known.

A religion subjected to such discipline could only exist if it had a set of special books in which the sacred traditions were faithfully preserved. These books existed, and are frequently mentioned by the Ancients. Authors often refer to *libri etrusci*, or *chartae etruscae* or *Etruscae disciplinae volumina*. These general terms comprise several types of series about which we know practically nothing except their titles, but whose contents can to some extent be guessed from these titles.

They include the *libri fatales,* collections of miracles, oracles, meteorological or astronomical phenomena—in brief, all the signs which could be considered as indications of the will of the gods, in other words, fate; the *libri Tagetici,* a kind of sacred code and collection of all the revelations attributed to the spirit Tages, comprising in essence the entire religious discipline, probably in metric form; the *libri Acheruntici,* attributed to Tages and perhaps forming part of the *libri Tagetici,* containing the doctrines of expiation and apotheosis, the rites for delaying the fulfilment of what has been fated, and methods of ensuring immortality for the souls of the departed through the blood of certain sacrifices offered to certain gods; and a series of more directly practical manuals such as (a) the *libri rituales,* laying down provisions for all aspects of public and private life, the founding of towns, the consecration of buildings, peace, war, the organization of society, the sacred chronology, birth, marriage and death; (b) the *libri fulgurales,* with the theory of thunderbolts and methods of observing and interpreting them; and (c) the *libri haruspicum,* with all the special science of haruspication.

All these sacred books were probably known and interpreted only by the families of lucumos, in the same way that pontifical law in Rome, up to a certain time, remained a closed sphere accessible only to patricians. A kind of home instruction existed in the great families, which ensured hereditary continuation of the sacred discipline and in which women could take part just as much as men—a perfectly natural situation in view of the status of women in the Etruscan family.

Some parts of the discipline, however, seem not to have been secret and to have been taught publicly. In particular, it seems that the science of haruspication was not confined to the families of lucumos.

123

*Priest at an altar
(6th century BC,
Cerveteri).*

9. The art of divination

Our knowledge of Etruscan divination comes mainly from the public or private use made of it by the Romans, and from information dating back no further than the time of Cicero and Varro, i.e. an era in which the traditions and languages of Etruria were only known to a few scholars. It comprised a body of doctrine supposedly revealed to the Etruscan lucumos by the spirit Tages and set out, together with some additions emanating from the nymph Vegon or Begoe—a kind of Tuscan Egeria or Sibyl—in a series of hieratic books which are mentioned, in their entirety or in part, under a number of different headings. From the first century BC on, this collection of arcana was translated into Latin, made the subject of commentaries and analyzed by various authors, one of whom is supposed to have written a fifteen-volume description of Etruscan doctrines. All these commentators and popularizers infused their own ideas and the theological, philosophical and scientific systems in fashion at the time into a tradition which was already partly apocryphal, artificially aged and overloaded. In addition, all that remains of their lucubrations are scattered fragments, too mutilated and incoherent to enable us, by comparing the parts common to them, to discover the body of doctrine with which they dealt or, still more, to separate purely Etruscan elements from exotic additions and adaptations. Under these circumstances, the best thing would be to stick to the historical facts which testify through the ages to the exercise of Etruscan divination: but these facts themselves cannot be understood without a framework of systematic concepts and general rules in which we shall try to place them.

There is no point in attempting a classification according either to the logical development of principles or to the historical vestiges of their application. There is only one established fact: inner revelation had no part in Tuscan divination, which was completely *inductive,* concerned solely with the interpretation of external signs.

These external signs of divine thought were necessarily situated in space, and a substantial part of their significance therefore derived from their location in relation either to parts of the visible world or to the observer. Thus, for divination to be possible, the area in which signs would appear had to be divided into segments in advance. This divided space was called the *templum,* or temple. The only individual property was therefore that which was designated by markings in conformity with the ritual, and a city could be truly founded only on land converted into a temple by the ceremonies held at its establishment.

The Romans attributed the origin of these concepts, which in their most rudimentary form were common to all ancient Italic peoples, to the Etruscans, and we know that they were used by augurs not only in dividing up the land but also in the distribution of the inhabitants of the city. The methods to be used for these complex calculations were set out in the *libri rituales.* "This name is used", says Festus, "for Etruscan books which lay down: the rites according to which towns must be founded and altars and buildings consecrated; the deity which protects the ramparts and the laws applicable to the gates; the proper distribution of tribes, curiae and centuries, the correct constitution and disposition of armies, and other similar rules governing both war and peace." The contemporaries of Augustus believed that

Etruscan vase in the Greek style (Vatican).

Roman haruspex consulting the entrails of a bull in accordance with Etruscan tradition (Capitol Museum, Rome).

their augural and pontifical law derived from the earlier and superior science of the Tuscans.

Originally, there was probably no basic difference between the Etruscan and the Roman temple. Like the augurs, the haruspices divided visible space, celestial and earthly, into four parts or quadrants by two straight lines from the cardinal points, perpendicular to each other and intersecting at the point at which the observer stood. The observer could then look along one of these lines and distinguish the left and the right, the foreground and the background of the temple.

The originality of the Etruscan temple lies in a matter of principle. Whereas the Romans, simplifying or not wishing to complicate tradition, considered all the signs appearing in the augural temple as having been sent by Jupiter alone, the haruspices claimed to be entering into communication with several deities and to recognize the hand from which the prophetic signs emanated. As a result, they located different deities in the various sectors of their temple; the number of such deities, and consequently the number of sectors, was bound to increase as the art of divination became more exact. And so the quadripartite temples, around which were located Jupiter, Juno, Summanus and Minerva, hurling their thunderbolts from their respective homes, were succeeded by temples with eight, twelve and sixteen sectors.

The eight-sector temple is assumed to have existed because of the sixteen-segment temple—of which there is explicit evidence—which must have evolved, as Cicero believed, as a result of repeated doubling of the parts of the primitive temple. This system perhaps accounts for the attribution (otherwise unexplained) of thunderbolts to nine divinities and—since time was divided like space—the *nundinum* or Etruscan week, as well as the eight successive races of men which, according to the haruspices, were to dominate the world.

It may legitimately be assumed that there was a twelve-sector temple, a more or less artificial imitation of the astrological Zodiac, which would have been the home of the twelve *consentes* or *complices*. These twelve "advisers" of Jupiter would have had to be armed with thunderbolts, but all we know about them is the monotheistically-inclined theory under which only Jupiter possessed thunderbolts. Even

the Romans did not go this far in simplifying the question of thunderbolts, since they attributed diurnal thunderbolts to Jupiter and nocturnal ones to Summanus. Innovators made a point of stating that they would restore primitive tradition on this point. In any event, they introduced rather incoherent ideas into the theory. Their view was that Jupiter had three thunderbolts *(tres manubiae)*. He could hurl the first one at his own initiative as a warning. If he wished to strike a second time, with greater force, he had to seek the opinion of the twelve *consentes*; he was not permitted, and probably could, not, hurl a third thunderbolt, this time in earnest, without consulting the "higher, veiled" gods. These six pairs of advisers are reminiscent both of the Olympians and the "adviser-gods" of Chaldea.

But this complex theory took no account of the requirements of existing practice, under which thunderbolts were localized within the temple and which was much more suited to various deities hurling thunderbolts from their various homes. The haruspices who preferred to develop national tradition from within had merely to increase the number of fulminant gods by adding to the old four-sector list the names of Vulcan, Mars, perhaps Hercules and others still unknown to us. As stated above, they thus reached the figure of 9. By combining this theory of nine fulminant gods with the theory of three thunderbolts described above, the Etruscans arrived at a figure of eleven different kinds of thunderbolt. It is not known whether or not this system was adapted to the use of a twelve-segment temple in which there was perhaps one empty space, corresponding to the area where, about the time of the winter solstice, lightning no longer struck from the sky but from earth. But it is certain that these eleven kinds of thunderbolt existed at the time of the sixteen-sector temple, the most typical fulgural temple and the only one whose existence is guaranteed by formal texts.

There was no need to prove that lightning was put forth by the gods. This assumption, which was common to all methods of divination, derived special strength from the difficulty which always faced physicians in explaining how fire, which naturally tends to rise, could rush so violently in the opposite direction.

The first question related to the origin of lightning, and it was more or less solved in advance by the position of the fulminant gods within the temple. Further indications were obtained from the *color* of the lightning, with bright red denoting the hand of Jupiter, dark red that of Mars and white of varying brilliance that of other gods; from its *timing:* daytime, nighttime or twilight; from its coincidence with the feasts of the various deities; and from its effects: a thunderbolt from Mars, for example, could be recognized by its combustive power. But it was not only to find out who had hurled the thunderbolt that the haruspices tried to ascertain its point of departure. They had to note its direction, both coming and going, for the Ancients, confused over phenomena which are not well understood even today, believed that lightning usually bounced off its target to disappear elsewhere or even return to its point of departure. All heavenly thunderbolts followed an oblique course; only those starting from earth struck in a straight line. The latter always presaged death, the former could be good or evil omens as the case might be. Thunderbolts hurled from the first quadrant of the temple (between North and East) were beneficial,

An augur: his curved staff enabled
him to fix the area of the sky in which
he would observe the flight of birds
(Uffici Museum, Florence).

especially if they returned there, for
such a return to the point of departure
was always a favorable sign.

The material effects of the lightning
were bound to constitute an important
method of diagnosis, since they could
reveal not only its origin but also the
intention which it signified. The
haruspices, with rather too much
assistance in their classification from
the Stoics, recognized three kinds of
thunderbolt: piercing, breaking and
burning, the last category being sub-
divided into those which merely
charred, i.e. changed the color of the
objects which they struck, and burning
thunderbolts proper which burned down
or set alight their targets.

This trichotomy, symbolized by the
three tongues of the classical thunderbolt, is found again when we come to
analyze other elements or methods of
description. The three thunderbolts
wielded by Jupiter, with or without the
help of the *consentes,* do not correspond
exactly to the above categories, since
they are specified in regard both to
their effects and to their intention
(warning, threat, execution). Another
approach classified thunderbolts as
frightening or destroying, a grouping
which is closer to the earlier one.

132

The distinctions were further refined through analysis. Celestial decrees could be repeated and confirmed, or they could be revoked by counter-orders. Whether opinions or threats, thunderbolts could presage inevitable ill-fortune, sometimes disguised as the promise of seeming happiness, including even exile or death, or else adversity which could be either eliminated or delayed. Thunderbolts were either perpetual, finite or prorogative. The first kind, like the astrologer's horoscope, influenced the whole life of individuals or cities. They were only to be seen at critical periods, and the haruspices, wanting to limit the share attributed to fatalism, had restricted the number of such periods to one for cities (the time of their foundation) and two for individuals (birth and the founding of a family). "Finite" thunderbolts related to happenings on a fixed date. The fulfilment of the "prorogative" prophesy, on the other hand, could be postponed for a certain time, not more than thirty years for cities and ten years for individuals, by means of a "procuration" indicated by the haruspice. This flexibility of Fate is a charactistic feature of Tuscan doctrine by comparison with astrology.

It has been assumed so far that the subjects of the omens were known, for the destination of thunderbolts was indicated by the time and place at which they were hurled. No doubt this was possible for thunderbolts which were requested, expected or observed. But these cases were rare. For others, the destination was deduced either from the existence of a preoccupation in the spectator, if lightning flashed but did not strike, or, with absolute certainty, from the site struck: property or the person himself, in the case of individuals; public places and monuments or magistrates, in the case of cities. In a republican city, thunderbolts striking "major sites" indicated both their destination and their meaning: these prodigious thunderbolts presaged revolutions leading to monarchy. Critics asked what was the purpose of thunderbolts which fell on *res nullius*—the sea, deserts, mountain-tops—and believed that this proved that they were not sent by the hands of the gods. This argument was easily refuted. If they were not seen, such thunderbolts did not exist; if they were, they were sent to whoever observed them. In any event, those who asked why the gods struck their own temples appeared to be unaware that these supposedly random strikes were the most significant of all. The haruspices usually interpreted them as *postularia* or *postulatoria,* prohibiting the continuation of wrongly executed religious ceremonies.

But all this casuistry meant little to the clients of the haruspices. What was expected of them was that they should indicate the steps to be taken to prevent any untoward consequences, by means of procuration.

The ancient Roman rite of Numa comprised only one uniform expiation which was applied by the Pontiffs to all thunderbolts. It consisted of symbolic offerings to Jupiter. The Pontiffs themselves admitted the inadequacy of this procedure and ended up by shifting the responsibility for purifying places and objects struck by lightning entirely onto the haruspices. According to a principle said to be common to the doctrine of Pontiffs and haruspices, thunderbolts only struck places which were sullied by some blemish. Interpretation was directed at discovering what this pre-existing blemish was, and the procuration ordered as a result was intended to have the effect of eradicating it.

But the evil brought by the thunderbolt itself to the place which it struck had first to be exorcised. This the haruspices did by burying the thunderbolt on the spot. They began by "gathering the heavenly fires", i.e. the material signs of their coming, and the thunderbolt itself, which they always managed to find burned out and solidified into stone. They then buried this thunderbolt, reciting baleful prayers, and interred with it one or more sheep *(bidentes),* whose entrails they were careful to examine to make sure that the operation would be a success. Lastly, they closed off this thunderbolt-tomb or *bidental* with a circular barrier like a well *(puteal):* it was now inviolable, fixed and classed, like all tombs, as a "religious" site.

If someone had died, the haruspices also "collected" the members of the person struck by lightning and buried them in the same place, without the consoling rites of a "just funeral". This type of *bidental* was therefore especially sinister. Trees struck by lightning, which remained standing like burial steles, stark and feared, were also treated in the same fashion.

The observance of these rites gave rise to many difficulties which pontifical law had to overcome. The theory of thunderbolts which returned to their point of origin made it possible to have fewer *bidentalia,* and may have been invented for that purpose. Only thunderbolts which remained on earth were buried. But the case of a person struck dead by lightning could prove embarrassing. If a person was struck in a public place, Tuscan ritual required that he should be buried on the spot, but Roman law forbade the conversion of a public place into a private burial-ground. If this public place was inside a town the difficulty was compounded, since one article of the law of the 12 Tables prohibited the burial of a human body *in urbe.* And what if the person survived? Should he be removed from society, or buried in effigy, as was done with "devotees", or should one affect optimism and regard a strike which did not kill as merely a caress? Even plant life caused doubts. Since the "religious" nature of trees struck by lightning was incompatible in pontifical law with being sacred, what should be done if lightning struck a sacred tree? In this case, the priests resorted to various rites by which the tree affected could be removed and replaced by another. Plants and trees could also survive a thunderbolt. If this happened, they were not made "religious" objects, but it was wise to regard them as being suspect and, in the case of fruit-trees, not to offer their fruits to the gods. Thus, Pliny relates that it was forbidden to pour libations with wine from a vine struck by lightning.

Before acquiring a reputation as eminent interpreters of thunderbolts, Tuscan augurs were known to be peerless in the art of examining entrails. Their usual name derives from this special part of their art, which was acknowledged to come from Tages, whereas the art of interpreting thunderbolts arose also—or perhaps exclusively—from the revelations of the nymph Vegon. A coin appears to represent Tages, wearing the haruspex's cap, and the instruments of the sacrificer. It may be compared with a bronze statuette found in a tomb near the Tiber, which gives a general picture of a haruspex.

Etruscan sacrificial rites did not possess any special principles or methods of their own. There was agreement everywhere that victims offered to the gods must be healthy and well-formed, and that the slightest blemish, visible or revealed by autopsy, prevented their approval.

Like the science of thunderbolts, haruspication finally became weighed down by supererogations caused by competition from astrology. The dissected animal had to become a microcosm and its entrails a temple around which the influences of the various deities were distributed; alternatively, the liver, the supreme organ of divination, was a temple in itself (the Ancients regarded the liver, not the heart, as the seat of life).

The haruspices applied their art to victims specially killed for the consultation: others counted only as sacrificial offerings, not as instruments of divination. Certain species were more sensitive to divine influence, their livers were "more eloquent". The idea was therefore conceived not of dissecting all animal species—including, it is said, man—but of adapting the species to the type of consultation, for example, by choosing a dove for lovers and so forth. But these techniques were only used by augurs of foreign origin: nothing indicates that the Tuscans added more augural animals to the list, like the Cypriots, who consulted the

Etruscan bronze depicting a sheep's liver, with annotations at the bottom (Piacenza Museum).

136

entrails of pigs, or Thrasybulus, who was the first to try a dog.

Nor do we know whether the number of entrails which could be examined, called *extra*—the liver, the heart, the lungs, the stomach, the spleen and the two kidneys—was brought up to seven by the Tuscans. All we know is that they were originally fewer, and that the additions caused quite a stir. Pliny notes the date (274) at which "the haruspices began to examine the heart among the *extra*."

Until then they no doubt had confined themselves to an inspection of the liver. At Cicero's time, the liver was not yet the complex temple it was later to become. The haruspices divided it summarily into four parts similar to the quadrants of the ancient temple. To do this, they merely had to supplement the natural division into two lobes—right and left—by an artificial division into two further parts, front and back, one of which was supposed to represent the interests of the observer or his clients, and the other conflicting interests and influences. The Tuscans observed mainly the protruding extremities of the organ (*fibrae*) and their fissures. The most important of the *fibrae* was the head

137

(caput) of the liver, which might be atrophied or missing, swollen or double, cohesive or detached; in all cases, it took precedence over or canceled out the omens of the other areas. Some augurs devoted special attention to the fissures, which may be compared with the "lines" of palmistry, or to combinations of fissures and veins. Obviously, anomalies of varying kinds—double livers, double sacs, livers situated where the spleen should be, double gall-bladders etc.—were noted with particular care. After the liver came the heart. It seems that a little fat at the top was a good omen. A missing heart was even rarer and, if possible, even more ominous, than a missing head in the liver; it was among the signs presaging Caesar's death. Understandably, this did not worry him much, since he regarded such prodigies as hoaxes. The lung also deserved attention: even if the other *extra* were favorable, an "incised" lung meant that any undertaking must be postponed.

All we know about the other *extra* is that the spleen and the liver sometimes miraculously changed places.

The haruspices used anatomical observations to amplify and correct the general prophesy which they made on the basis on a first glance at the still warm entrails, and they even used the attitude of the victim before death to help them. Seneca and Lucan give lengthy and pretentious descriptions of all that they knew about bad omens in international haruspication: unwillingness of the victim; long and convulsive agony; black blood flowing instead of spurting out; pallid color and blemishes on entrails not in their normal place and bathed in bloody pus; spilled bile, torn and gaping intestines; liver with double and detached head, clogged lungs, flabby heart and other terrifying conditions.

But the observations described so far were more or less common to all augurs, and any differences were of interpretation. What was peculiar to the Tuscan rite was the additional information obtained by cooking the entrails. After the autopsy, the Greeks observed the effects of burning the entrails and flesh in the hearth. They burned the divine part and only boiled the human part. The Tuscans, on the other hand, boiled the augural entrails for a long time before eating them. It sometimes happened that the head of the liver, or even the entire liver itself, dissolved, and this was naturally

A sacrifice. The grief of a mother or sister.

an omen of death.

Consultative sacrifices could be made at any time at the request of and paid for by the State or individuals. In addition to requests resulting from random happenings, the Roman Pontiffs considered it appropriate to introduce regular consultations without any specific purpose, as opportunities offered to the gods to manifest their goodwill. Eight times a year (on January 10 and 14, February 16 and 26, March 13 August 22, October 14 and December 12) day-long sacrifices were offered: the victims were killed in the morning and the entrails cremated in the evening.

Unrivaled in the art of interpreting thunderbolts and in haruspication, the Tuscans were also past masters in the art of interpreting and "procuring" inexplicable events or prodigies.

A prodigy, whatever it was called *(prodigium, miraculum)*, was something which could not be entirely explained by known causes and which could therefore reveal its unknown cause to those skilled in the art.

Because it was always fortuitous, it could not be the subject of intentional and well-prepared observation. The task of the haruspices was to interpret it in the light of their findings or testimony and, if requested, to indicate the appropriate type of procuration. As a guarantee of their competence they could point to long experience, set out in special volumes *(ostentaria)*. This mass of details, gathered in a country said to be particularly rich in miracles, was classified according to the object concerned. Tarquitius, the translator of the *Ostentarium Tuscum*, at least, was responsible for an *Ostentarium arborarium*, and there was another special book concerning a ram with a purple fleece, in other words, prodigies which occurred in the animal kingdom.

Just as thunderbolts which "remained on earth" entailed a predetermined expiation, which was independent of their interpretation, so prodigies in a material object required a similar operation consisting of ridding the city of the monster concerned. As the sign—and with it the portent—could not be transported elsewhere without causing disputes, it was drowned in the sea or destroyed by fire. In 207 BC, when a hermaphrodite as large as a four-year old child was born at Frusinone, the haruspices decided that it must be put into a box and thrown far out to sea, so that it could not contaminate the ground by coming into contact with it.

The Roman penal code, which was completely derived from theology, treated moral monsters, parricides, in the same way. They were sown in a bag with a dog, a cock, a viper and a monkey and thrown into the sea. The mention of a monkey, which the Etruscans might have encountered earlier, together with the fact .that Strabo knew the Etruscan word for monkey, suggests that the Roman law was drawn up or reformulated after consultation with the haruspices. It may also be suspected that the Etruscans had a hand in the horrible provision that Vestal Virgins guilty of incest should be buried alive, since their offense was regarded as being a prodigy. The books of Tages seem to have classed as prodigies all crimes which could be defined as sacrilege.

These books stated that the descendants of perjurers must be expelled, implying a still more severe penalty for the perjurers themselves.

In times of crisis, intense concern increased the number of prodigies. When the crisis had passed, the people forgot its terror and believed that it had warded off the effects or exhausted the consequences of supernatural signs. But the science of the haruspices went still further. They could distinguish the conditional from the inevitable and, in what was inevitable, separate what could be postponed from what was bound to occur at a fixed time. Where the layman had seen only change happenings, they recognized from time to time an event which had been expected and formed part of an overall plan, a predestined stage in the life of individuals or societies. These high-flown speculations, which were the result mainly of the rival influence of astrology, were ascribed, as always, to Tages, the author responsible for all the fantasises of his disciples. They were contained in the *libri fatales*.

With regard to individuals, Tuscan tradition was clearly able to provide only general indications. In the *Etrusci libri fatales*, Varro had found a certain biological and theological system, whose structure he may have altered by introducing alien calculations. According to Varro's incomplete and mutilated account, it was possible, by using the religious rites as a prayer, to postpone fatal events up to the age of seventy; thereafter, one could no longer request such postponement and could not obtain it from the gods. After the age of eighty-four, men lost their minds and prodigies no longer occurred for them.

The multiples of 12 and 7 used here betray the intrusion of astrology, or at least the astrological ideas current in Greece since the time of Solon. We also know that the peripatetic philosopher Staseas of Naples professed ideas attributed by Varro to the Etruscans with respect to the nullity of existence prolonged beyond the normal span. What was particular to the haruspices was the theory of prorogation of events and also, probably, the mobility of the limits marking the various stages of life. These stages, which the Greeks called "climacterics" and determined in advance by mathematics, were recognized by their Tuscan rivals in certain prodigies which were sent at an appropriate time by the gods, the masters of speeding up or slowing down time. The original idea of regarding old men who continued to live despite their years as walking corpses must have been a compromise, perhaps worked out by Staseas, between astrology and haruspication. As the twelve astrological periods totaled 84 years, and haruspication taught that postponements obtained by individuals were valid for ten years, it was presumably useless to request delays after the age of 74, since the remainder of life was at most enough for the postponements granted in the ten previous years.

It may be supposed that the usual doctrine was kinder and that it even allowed debts contracted in this world to be paid in the next. What Jupiter could no longer grant was requested from the "Fates".

If redemption through sacrifice could exempt one from the evils of this world, why could it not also do so from the evils beyond the grave? When the mystic religions were dangling the path of immortality before their adherents, the haruspices seem to have outbid their competitors, who promised the joy of immortality only to those who had prepared for it during their lifetime. "Etruria", says Arnobius, "promises in its books that souls become divine and are freed from the laws of mortality by offering the blood of certain animals to certain deities."

When applied to the life of cities rather than individuals, Etruscan doctrines are more comprehensible. There can be no doubt that the haruspices claimed to have in their archives prophesies about the fate of certain towns, since the *libri fatales* or *fata scripta* of the people of Veii specify the circumstances in which Veii would be captured and conditionally announce the conquest of Rome by the Gauls as a result of the capture of Veii.

This survey would be incomplete if it did not mention the interpretation of flights of birds or of certain rains. A fresco on a tomb at Vulci shows a divination scene, in which two men are keeping careful watch. One is anxiously and rather impatiently observing a bird: he would like to make it take flight. The other has methodically fixed a point in the sky according to the rules of the haruspices and is waiting for the bird, passing before him, to determine the omen by the direction of its flight.

It should also be noted that in the 3rd century the Etruscans seem to have had some contacts with the famous Chaldean magi and to have learned some secrets and mysteries from them. This perhaps strengthened the influence of astrology on their traditional beliefs.

The domestic history of Etruria is a closed book. The aristocracy of the lucumos probably acted as the repository for priestly traditions and, in particular, the secrets of divination revealed by Tages. This caste, in which women participated in the exercise of the augural art, was forced gradually to grant access to theological and ritual studies to lower classes— and even to foreigners—to take less and less interest in divination as it became a profession and, finally, to disappear, leaving in its place schools or groups of haruspices following an aged leader.

Whatever their beliefs and mysterious practices, the Etruscans nevertheless lived their lives basically in the same way as all other men. And since—quite reasonably—they thought about death so much, it should be said that death was for them the same as it is for all beings: the favorite subjects for their sculptors of urns and sarcophagi were those which express, more or less obliquely, the heartbreak of separation, the sudden blow which strikes men in the midst of their affections and their joys, the mysterious force which tears them away from life and transports them to an unknown world. Sometimes they depicted the agony of a dying man surrounded by his tearful family. Sometimes they showed a final farewell, the last embrace of man and wife, two friends, a father and child. The horse of death whose task is to bear the dead man to his underworld abode stands by, ready to leave. It leaves, and the separation is complete.

When the inevitable time had passed, when these agonizing moments had gone, special festivals were held. The fact that life is short encouraged men to live it to the full and to celebrate the miracle of existence. Dances and games usually accompanied a funeral. The procession included trumpets. Sometimes an actor in a chariot represented the dead man. Religious as it was, the life of an Etruscan man comprised above all the joys and sorrows of men of all times.

143

Credits : Alinari/V : 70, 72, 81 b, 97 b, 103 b, 116, 119, 143 — Anderson/V : 25, 44, 50, 57 b, 58, 60, 61 a, b, 64, 67, 68, 69, 74, 75, 79, 81 c, 112 b, 114 a — Archives : 8, 42, 43, 54, 137 — Giraudon : 2, 18, 26, 56, 57 a, 76 a, b, 77 a, b, 97 a, 101, 102, 104, 112 a, 124, 128 — Lauros/Giraudon : 36, 110 — R.L. : 139 — Scala : 17, 35, 53, 71, 73, 91, 109, 127 — Viollet : 7, 10, 13, 15, 19, 20, 29, 31, 32, 38, 40, 45, 63, 65, 81 a, 83, 84, 85, 86, 88, 89, 92, 93, 94, 95 a, b, 96 a, 98, 100, 103 a, 107.

Printer, Industria Gráfica. S.A.   Barcelona
Depósito legal B. 41117-1973
Printed in Spain 1973